# Chivalry and Romance

# Chivalry and Romance

## Vignettes from Indian History and Bardic Legends

E. Jaiwant Paul

NIYOGI
BOOKS

Published by
NIYOGI BOOKS
D-78, Okhla Industrial Area, Phase-I
New Delhi-110 020, INDIA
Tel: 91-11-26816301, 49327000
Fax: 91-11-26810483, 26813830
email: niyogibooks@gmail.com
website: www.niyogibooksindia.com



Editor: Shaurya Shaukat Sircar / Niyogi Books
Design: Arrt Creations, Nabanita Das / Niyogi Books

ISBN: 978-93-81523-89-6
Year of Publication: 2013

This book is a work of historical fiction. As history, every effort has been made to accurately reflect the dates, places and events where the cited historical figures appeared. Although it draws from historical records and bardic legends, its purpose is not to answer historical questions or settle historical controversies. As fiction, many of the words and actions of these figures are drawn solely from the author's imagination and therefore reflect only what might have been said or done at these events.



Printed at: Niyogi Offset Pvt. Ltd., New Delhi, India

*For*

Shubh, Nisha, Viveka,
Karan, Subroto,
Kabir, Abhay,
Ishan and Mihir.

# Contents

# Introduction

This collection of stories ranges from prehistoric times to as recently as the last century. Those of ancient times are based more on bardic legends, but as we progress in time, there is greater historic fidelity of events. These accounts are not arranged in a chronological order as each has a flavour independent of the other. The common link however is that they are all based on dramatic events of history or on epic poems of great bards like Chand Bardai, Lal Kavi, Sukhdharma and others. Some however are sourced from a combination of both history and bardic legends. The markers of history are kept in mind even when these accounts are enlivened by bardic poems.

The discovery of historical facts is scientific in method. But history tends to be dry, unless it is embellished and supported by great literature. On the other hand ballads can be soul stirring and bring tears to your eyes, which history seldom does.

Bards were attached to the courts of Indian kings. In Rajasthan, Bundelkhand and Saurashtra, bards were even considered a sacred order and as hereditary guardians of history and pedigree. They were treated with great respect by the kings and were esteemed higher than Brahmins. As Colonel Tod says in his *Annals and Antiquities of Rajasthan*, 'The Rajput attends more to the martial song of the bard than to the litany of the Brahmin.' In some states rulers used to rise when one of their order entered or left an assembly. Bards often accompanied kings during wars and thus their reporting was first hand.

Bards have been called 'the historians of mankind'. They are essentially historians, genealogists and reciters of warlike poetry. Much would have been lost but for the bards and *charans* whose epics are passed down from generation to generation. Thus traditions have been kept alive. They wrote impassioned verse about war, bravery, love, loyalty, great deeds, glory, sacrifice and death. The language was flowery and prone to hyperbole. Their poems may not always be historically reliable but they are always inspiring, fiery and full of passion.

The accounts in this book relate to characters, some well known in history and others equally fascinating to whom history has paid scant attention, possibly because enough is not known about them. The latter are footnotes or disposed off in a short paragraph in history books although their lives are as captivating.

On occasion I have included the original language of the poetic bards. The drama cannot always be reduced to the severe style of history. The original bardic texts retain the chivalry and the romance and hence their inclusion.

# 1

# The Beautiful Mastani

M*astani*, the exact translation of the word is difficult. It is a combination of spirited and exciting. And I may still be wrong.

I have seen a few paintings of her in various households. They are old and show much wear and tear, but most are beautifully executed on layers of paper stuck together or on glass. The face is remarkably similar in all of them suggesting that it may be close to the original. It is a three quarters view of the face, not the profile as was the common practice then. The eyes are wide open and striking, the lips thin, an unremarkable nose, a well-moulded chin and a long slender neck. She wears an odd-shaped headgear and little jewellery. An attractive, arresting face, almost beautiful. I have asked the owners of the paintings about her but they know little. 'A wife or the mistress of one of the kings of central India.' And that was about all.

There was something intriguing about the woman, something mysterious, and I was curious. It was easy to find that she was the mistress of the great warrior Peshwa, Baji Rao. I scoured the libraries, I sought help at the National Archives, and even traced and communicated with one of Baji Rao's decendants, who now lives in Pune.

I found precious little. But let us put together what my efforts unearthed, which I think, is more than you would find elsewhere.

Baji Rao was the great Maratha general who in the mid-eighteenth century changed the map of India. He transformed the Maratha nation state into an empire, conquering Malwa, Gujarat, Bundelkhand and large tracts in the Deccan. Born with a sword in his hand, his life was war and he spent it on the battlefield or in a camp or on the horseback. Brave as a tiger and handsome as a god, Baji Rao became a legend while still very young and tragically died while still in his prime. He raided Mughal Delhi and swore he would plant his flag across the river Indus. Death robbed him of this honour, but his son fulfilled his pledge in 1758.

Mastani was the love of Baji Rao's life. She came to him when he was thirty-one years old and stayed by his side till his death, and it may be said, even beyond. She lived with him at his Shaniwar Palace at Pune. She rode with him stirrup to stirrup on his numerous campaigns; she was his inspiration in battle; she was the mother of his son and when he finally died, she fearlessly chose to perish in the flames. Mastani was also the single biggest complication in Baji Rao's personal life: she was a Muslim.

Although Mastani was such a vital part of Baji Rao's life, she remains elusive as facts about her are scarce. Most historians have almost nothing to say about her, some dismiss her in a single sentence while others have given her a paragraph, at most a page. Perhaps they swept her under the carpet because she was an embarrassment, a woman everyone frowned upon. There are some references to Mastani in contemporary letters but they are difficult to come by. However, piecing together fleeting references to Mastani, an ephemeral and dreamlike form emerges.

Who was Mastani? Even that question remains unanswered, although according to the distinguished historian D.B. Parasnis, the most acceptable theory is that she was the daughter of the great Chhattrasal of Bundelkhand from a Muslim mistress. Chhattrasal presented Mastani to Baji Rao along with one-third of his kingdom, when the Peshwa went to Chhattrasal's aid and repelled the Mughals from his dominions. This opinion is corroborated by an account given in a Maratha *bakhar* (chronicle).

In addition Parasnis refers to a genealogical account which he got directly from the descendants of Mastani, which support this belief. Pogson in his *A History of the Boondelas* (1828) also refers to Mastani as Chhattrasal's daughter. However, there is a second theory which is that Mastani was the daughter of Nizam-ul-Mulk who on the advice of his wife, presented her to Baji Rao after performing a mock ceremony of her marriage with a *khanjar* (dagger), hoping thereby to promote diplomatic relations with the Marathas. There are some other suppositions about Mastani's origin but they are too whimsical to be accepted.

The earliest reference to Mastani in historical records is in a letter dated 14 February 1830, containing a statement about the cost of the apparel and dresses presented to her on the occasion of the marriage of Baji Rao's eldest son. Thus the beautiful Mastani makes a dramatic entry on the great stage of Indian history, elegantly robed and raimented. Other historical references to Mastani are few and far between but all agree about her sharp wit and exquisite beauty. Mastani was as far-sighted as she was lovely and it is said, that initially she would not accept Baji Rao's advances, until he pledged that any son born of their union, would receive a fair share of his property. The young Peshwa fell deeply in love with her and Mastani with him. She rode a high horse and followed him on all his campaigns, which meant riding hundreds of miles over rugged country, living in camps under canvas and sharing his rough fare. Her daring and courage were no less than her beauty for she faced all the dangers of war. She never left his side and looked after Baji Rao with the devotion of a wife.

*Tarikh-i-Mohammad Shahi* mentions that Mastani was skilled in riding and was as good as any soldier in horsemanship, spear throwing and swordplay. This must have delighted Baji Rao's heart even more. Mention is also made in other texts of her talent for dancing and singing. At the annual Ganapati festival, Baji Rao used to hold a function where close friends were invited, and the main attraction was Mastani's singing and dancing. It seems strange though, and difficult to understand why Baji Rao allowed her to perform in public when she was so close to his heart.

As the years passed, the two became inseparable. On one occasion the Peshwa went so far as to forget etiquette and took her along with him to Satara, when he went to pay his respects to the king. Shahu was indignant and reprimanded him royally.

One brief statement by a Mughal commander is recorded and says much of Baji Rao and Mastani's closeness. Baji Rao's attack on the Imperial capital Delhi was a hazardous expedition, full of uncertainties but Mastani rode stirrup behind him. After this assault, Baji Rao withdrew his forces and a Mughal scout who had ridden ahead describes how he 'came upon Baji Rao and his mistress, seated on one saddle cover, drinking and singing while they rested'. There they were, returning from a perilous and hard fought battle, having ridden over 60 kilometres that day, sitting and enjoying themselves like young lovers on a picnic.

The path of true love, however, is never smooth. Baji Rao's wife, Kashi Bai, was a most respected and suitable lady, but his mistress, Mastani (and mistresses are never suitable or respected) complicated his life no end, but then she was the one he loved. Baji Rao grew distant from his wife, and neglected her regularly. This naturally distressed his son Balaji, his brother Chimnaji and his mother Radha Bai. They protested most strongly at the relationship but Baji Rao ignored all of them. Sometime later the three got together and while Baji Rao was out on a campaign, they removed Mastani by force and imprisoned her in a distant house, which was strongly guarded. In response she went on a hunger strike to protest her confinement. But that did not work, so the high-spirited woman that she was, she planned an escape. She studied the positioning of the guards, the layout of the house and particularly the stabling of the horses. One night she outwitted the captors, got hold of a fleet horse and galloped off into the darkness. She rejoined her lover who was camping near Patas. This confinement of Mastani by his family behind his back deeply wounded Baji Rao.

Years later when Baji Rao was away fighting, what turned out to be his last war, the orthodox section of Brahmins and some among the nobility considered the possibility of murdering Mastani. This was however, much too risky; Baji Rao was after all a dominating figure, and so they sounded the king about their heinous plan. Shahu forbade it totally; he was also against forcible separation or any form of personal restraint. He refused to tolerate any action that might be offensive to Baji Rao. He wrote, 'On no account can there be any offence to the feelings of Baji Rao. The evil does not abide in the lady. The relationship can be broken only when Baji Rao is so inclined.'

The nobility next made Baji Rao a topic of public criticism. The priests among them refused to officiate at the thread ceremony of one of his sons and the marriage of a relative, if Baji Rao was present. They protested, 'How can we perform these rites when a tainted man, who eats meat and drinks wine and lives with a Muslim woman, is present.' For these men these prejudices were all important and his great victories, his valour and the glory he had brought to his people were as naught.

*Baji Rao*

In 1734, Mastani bore Baji Rao's son. This thawed the icy coldness of the Peshwa's family towards Mastani slightly. Soon he added a new wing to the Shaniwar Palace, solely for her and her son.

Baji Rao's ardent desire was that his son by Mastani should be declared a Brahmin. But it is a telling commentary on the vice-like grip that the orthodox Brahmins and the priesthood had, that even a powerful man like Baji Rao could not break through the opposition. Hinduism accepts no converts and the son of a Muslim courtesan could never be invested with the sacred thread. At last they had their revenge and finally, Baji Rao with a heavy heart, was forced to bring up his son as a Muslim. Here was the champion of Hinduism, who the Mughals wrongly believed wanted to root out Islam from India, being forced by orthodox sections to bring up his son as per the traditions of Islam. The boy was named Shamsher Bahadur, an apt name for a son of the great warrior.

Not surprisingly, Shamsher Bahadur was brought up by Baji Rao to be a soldier. He grew up to be admired for his ardour and courage. At the age of twenty-seven, he fought bravely at Panipat and fell on the battlefield. Shamsher Bahadur left a son, Ali Bahadur, who inherited Baji Rao's lands in Bundelkhand, as per the promise given to Mastani. These included the towns of Kalpi and Banda and the environs, which Ali Bahadur extended, making himself master of a tract of country, establishing the state of Banda. His descendant, the Nawab of Banda, true to his ancestry, fought side by side with Lakshmi Bai, Rani of Jhansi, and the Maratha chief, Rao Saheb, against the British in the Revolt of 1857. The Nawab of Banda came to the rani's help at the Battle of Kalpi with cavalry and a supply of cannons. After their defeat there, he fought by her side again at the final battle at Gwalior. In that battle, the rani fell fighting while the nawab lost an arm. He later took advantage of the amnesty offered by the British.

However, to return to Baji Rao, during the last few months before his premature death, there was trouble again in the family about Mastani. Details are sketchy but it appears that some of the family succeeded in separating Baji Rao from Mastani. At this stage, it appears that Baji Rao considered the use of armed force but did not resort to it in order to avoid domestic strife. Weary of the struggle, he decided to seek on the battlefield that peace of mind which he could not find in his own home. This was the last campaign that Baji Rao undertook in 1740 against the Nizam, but even after winning this final round against the Nizam, Baji Rao did not return to Pune, probably because of the trouble he was having with the closest members of his family. Instead, he chose to go and inspect his *jagirs* at Khargone near Indore. A letter dated 7 March 1740, from Chimnaji to Baji Rao's son shows that Baji Rao was sick at heart at the family quarrels and his disappointed passion. Baji Rao never met Mastani again. He suddenly fell ill with fever and died. Radha Bai, Chimnaji and his son Balaji, came to Khargone and with them came Mastani. No one had the slightest inkling of her intentions but at the cremation ceremony, she suddenly broke through the crowd and fearlessly, with a smile on her face, she walked into the sea of flames. Though still a young woman she chose to die in the most horrendous way. Before the stunned family could react or prevent her, the beautiful Mastani was gone. Separated from her lover in this world, she went to greet him in the next.

The palace where Mastani resided—the Shaniwar Palace—was built by Baji Rao at Pune ten years after his elevation to the office of Peshwa. As a result of a devastating fire which broke out in February 1828, all the buildings within the walls were destroyed although the fortified outer walls survived.

The part of the palace and fortified walls which most excite human interest is the Mastani Gate, which led into the apartments especially built by Baji Rao for his beautiful and devoted mistress.

Mastani, as mentioned, committed sati on Baji Rao's funeral pyre. My search for her however reveals a second version of her end. According to this, when news of the Peshwa's death was received by Mastani, at the Shaniwar Palace in Pune, she committed suicide. She was buried at Pabal, around 30 kilometres east of Pune which is a village that Baji Rao had gifted her. Her unpretentious tomb there still reminds passers-by of her tragic love. But so much about Mastani is shrouded in mystery. We shall never know whether she committed sati at Rewar or whether she resorted to suicide at Pune. Either way she chose to die with her loved one.

2

# Rewriting History ~ Prithviraj Chauhan

Afghanistan—arid dusty plains, barren craggy mountains, interspersed surprisingly by fertile fruit bearing oases. It is not a country one would normally visit but work took me there a couple of times; the last trip being in 1972. The foreign invasions and the self destructive civil war lay in the future.

I was in Afghanistan to meet my counterparts from Pakistan. I used to work for a multinational company where it was considered useful to periodically meet colleagues from across the border. However relations between India and Pakistan being what they were, it was not practical to meet in each others' countries, so the venue used to be Kabul, Colombo or sometimes London.

Kabul had changed slightly from the last time I had been there a few years earlier, when it was literally a collection of mud huts. This time round it was still ramshackled and dusty but interestingly the front row of buildings on a few main roads were three or four storey high concrete structures. But behind this façade, the mud huts took over again with dirt roads and overflowing open drains. Donkeys everywhere, carrying loads of fruit, vegetables, grain and kerosene oil.

The brown river Kabul slicing through the town with its very fragile and shaky pedestrian bridges.

The Afghans are a personable race, though they could all do with a good scrub and a wash, their turbans and their waistcoats are colourful. The women walked gingerly shrouded in their head-to-toe burqas, peering through the eye-slits.

We spent the next couple of days at the Intercontinental Hotel holding discussions with the Pakistanis, drinking good Scotch and eating tandoori kebabs. After the conference had ended and the Pakistanis had departed, I had scheduled a couple of days extra in Afghanistan, as I had work in Kandahar, which lies about 300 kilometres towards the south. The road was surprisingly good, having been built recently by German contractors. Our agent, an Indian settled there for decades, drove me down in his new Toyota.

About half way to Kandahar is the town of Ghazni. I was curious about the place, having read many references in history books, but it was a disappointment. Ghazni is a small dusty town with the ubiquitous mud huts and a sprinkling of brick buildings. The place is dominated by a small mud fort of no architectural significance. I did wonder about this anomaly that the Afghans, who built some imposing monuments in North India, had hardly any structure worth the name in their own country, not even an arched gateway. But on reflection, the answer to this is not far to seek.

On the outskirts of Ghazni, however, my eye was caught by two ancient domed buildings, which for a change were made of stone and were architecturally pleasing. They stood side-by-side, one larger than the other. The dome of the bigger monument was made of some greenish stone. Both had high arched entrances and were approached through a small garden. These were the only monuments of some note that I had seen in the country and I stopped to take a look. We entered the larger one and found that it was a tomb. One of the locals informed us that it was the tomb of Mohammad Ghori. The second tomb was smaller and not as refined in construction. The interior was bare and sunlight came in through the large arches. Coarse grass grew inside. In the centre there was a bare patch, where the actual grave should have been. Hanging over this spot, from the top of the dome was a long thick rope ending in a knot at shoulder height. As I stood there wondering, some local Afghans came in and went through a curious routine. They caught the knot at the end of the rope in one hand and stamped vigorously with one foot on the bare patch of earth where the grave was. I watched this repeated several times by different people and seeking an explanation I discovered an astounding fact; a fact that left me flabbergasted.

Here we have to pause and step back 900 years. Prithviraj Chauhan one of the most splendorous and charismatic kings was born in 1166. While still young, he extended his conquests over northern Rajasthan and Punjab. His territory then matched with that of Mohammad Ghori, who had occupied Lahore. There was however constant contact and commerce between the two kingdoms.

Prithviraj's pre-eminence in northern India had brought him in conflict with the powerful king of Kannauj, Jaichand. The latter's ambition to declare himself paramount sovereign by *ashwamedh* (the ceremony of the horse sacrifice) was thwarted by Prithviraj. The hostility was further intensified when Prithviraj carried off Jaichand's daughter Sanyogita from the *swayamvar* (bride's selection of a husband). This tale has been immortalised in Chand Bardai's *Prithvirajaraso*. To accomplish the downfall of his rival, Jaichand resorted to the dangerous expedient of asking for help from Mohammad Ghori.

Prithviraj Chauhan fought two battles against Ghori. The first battle was fought in 1191 at Tarain; located 150 kilometres south of Lahore, and was a result of Ghori storming the Fort of Bhatinda. Prithviraj hastened to its rescue and the ensuing battle has been described in lively detail. The battle joined as the Indians gave the signal for attack by blowing conch shells from the backs of elephants; while the Turks struck their kettle drums carried on camels and sounded their trumpets. The impetuous charge of the Rajputs scattered like a cloud the Muslim vanguard.

Advancing further, they attacked both wings of the Turkish army, dispersed their opponents and threatened the centre, where the sultan commanded in person. Large numbers of his horsemen began to slip away, not daring to face the roaring tide of Rajput cavalry flushed with victory. The sultan was urged to save himself by flight as he had no support left. But scorning such cowardly counsel, he made a reckless charge into the body of Rajputs before him, hewing his way with his sword, followed by a small body of devoted companions. Govind Rai, the governor of Delhi, who led the vanguard of his brother Prithviraj, on sighting Ghori from a distance, drove his elephants towards him. The two met in single combat. The Sultan's lance knocked out two of Govind Rai's front teeth, while the Indian chief hurled a javelin which inflicted a severe wound on the upper arm of Ghori and forced him to turn his horse's head round in agony and weakness. Barely able to keep his seat, Mohammad was saved by a brave Khalj youth, who leapt up behind him in the saddle and piloted him from the battle field carrying him away to the base. Seeing this, many from the Ghori troops feared the worst; they believed that their leader was dead and thus broke off the encounter. The high point of the battle was thus the personal contest between Govind Rai of Delhi and Mohammad of Ghor.

The rout of the Turkish army was complete, but such a victory did not yield its full fruit as the Rajputs could not pursue the retreating army as their country bred ponies were outrun by the Khurasani horses of the Turkish army and thus the enemy could withdraw in good order.

Mohammad Ghori returned to Ghazni to convalesce and swore to avenge this defeat. He assembled a vast force of Turks, Afghans, Persians and Arabs estimated at 120,000 cavalry clad in armour. But the most numerous and effective contingents were of Turkic stock.

The Rajput army was much smaller this time as Prithviraj had been disgracefully inactive and had delayed mobilising his forces. He was still in his mid-twenties and was said to be enjoying himself since his earlier victory. Many of his former allies, due to jealousy and revenge, did not join him and remained indifferent spectators. His long time rival Jaichand, the Raja of Kannauj, traitorously allied himself with Ghori.

Prithviraj asked his kinsman Samarsi, the wise and valiant king of Mewar, for assistance and though the latter read Prithviraj an indignant lecture on his lack of

*Prithviraj Chauhan*

*Mohammad Ghori*

preparation, he raised his buckler to defend Prithviraj.

The two armies came face to face again at Tarain. Here Prithviraj sent a friendly warning to Ghori to save his men's lives by withdrawing and he promised to allow Ghori safe passage. From a detailed account left by the historian Ferishta, there was much trickery on the part of Ghori. He responded to Prithviraj's suggestion of making peace on the condition that he is allowed possession of western Punjab while the rest of Hindustan would remain under the ruling kings. Pending Prithviraj's reply Ghori would suspend hostilities. Prithviraj foolishly fell for the ruse and the Rajputs conceiving that Mohammad had been intimidated, relaxed their vigil and spent the night in riot and revelry. It was early dawn of a winter's day and when the Indian soldiers woke in need of ablutions and breakfast, they found the Ghori forces already entering their lines. With sore heads and empty stomachs they had to snatch up their arms and form their lines as best as they could in a hurry.

Ghori launched wave after wave of mounted archers, who shot from a distance but did not try to force the Indian position and in fact feigned flight and retreat as

the Indian elephant phalanx and horses advanced. Prithviraj sensing success pressed on further, but the buffeting attacks of the Turkish horses took their toll on the all-night revelers. By sunset, Mohammad Ghori putting himself at the head of 12,000 superb horses, whose riders were covered with steel armour and making one desperate charge carried death and destruction in the Rajput ranks. It was a complete victory for the Turks.Govind Rai, the hero of the first battle at Tarain was slain; his body was recognised by the missing teeth. Samarsi, the king of Mewar, was also killed. History books record that the young and gallant Prithviraj Chauhan, who had changed his elephant for a horse was captured and executed in cold blood to appease Ghori's wrath.

There is however another version about Prithviraj's fate after the battle. No history records this version; they all say Prithviraj was slain. But Chand Bardai, the famous bard of Rajasthan has a different story to tell and bards, it has been said, 'are the historians of mankind'. In his 100,000 verse epic *Prithvirajaraso*, Chand Bardai states that Prithviraj was not killed in the battle. He was captured by Ghori's men and presented before the sultan. The latter delighted that he could now wreck his vengeance, took his adversary to Afghanistan. Here Ghori had Prithviraj's eyes put out and threw him into prison.

Prithviraj's prowess as an archer was legendary and though blinded he could still find his aim if given an indication of direction and distance. This never failed to astonish Ghori. Once the sultan asked Prithviraj to demonstrate his archery to visitors from North India, among whom was Chand Bardai. Just as Prithviraj was about to start, Chand recited a couplet:

*Char bans, Chaubis gaz, ungal asht pramaan*
*To Uchya baitho hai Sultan, mat chukyo Chauhan*

This gave Prithviraj the direction and distance at which Sultan Ghori sat. Chand added that if you are a Chauhan you will not miss him whereupon Prithviraj swung around and shot the arrow straight through Ghori's chest.

We now go back to November 1972. It was a cold day and I was standing inside a domed tomb with a thick rope hanging from the top and ending in a knot. The Afghans grab this knot in one hand and stamp vigorously and repeatedly on the bare patch of earth in the centre of the tomb. I seek an explanation for this strange routine and I discover the confounding fact that this is the tomb of the Indian King Prithviraj Chauhan.

The Afghans stamp on his grave to this day because he killed their great Sultan Mohammad Ghori 900 years ago. Prithviraj's tomb stands near Ghazni and I have been there. Indian history books need to be rewritten. Chand Bardai was recording an actual fact which is supported by Afghan history.

After the family of Afghans had left, I placed a flower on that bare patch of earth, but it must have soon been stamped upon.

His remains must be brought back home, where they belong.

# 3

# Maharana Pratap

We have a summer house in the Kumaon Himalayas. On one of our forays from there we went to Binsar, which at an attitude of 7,600 feet commands a magnificent view of the great peaks, Trisul and Nanda Devi. At the Khali Estate where we stayed, the Colonial bungalow was built in 1871. The Manager of the estate was very interesting and knowledgeable about local lore so I asked him his name, which he said was Bhama Shah. That rang a bell and I said, 'You don't happen to be from Mewar, do you?' He looked a bit surprised and replied, 'Indeed yes, but we have lived in Kumaon for a couple of generations now.' This was a coincidence and I asked, 'Was your ancestor by any chance the famous Bhama Shah of Mewar?' He was delighted that I knew and said, 'The very same.' He then regaled us with many a tale of his family and his ancestor, who through one selfless act had changed the very history of Rajasthan and Mughal India.

The third and last time that Chittorgarh was sacked, was in 1567 by Emperor Akbar. The details of this are mentioned elsewhere in this book. Rana Udai Singh who has been labelled 'The Craven Prince' fled to the sanctuary of the hills, an action out of character for a Rajput. Chittor, the thousand year old abode of kings was dishonoured and rendered desolate. As Colonel James Tod indignantly wrote, 'Well had it been for Mewar had the annals never recorded the name of Oody Singh in the catalogue of her princes.'

Udai Singh had several sons, the eldest of whom was Pratap. Udai Singh died at the early age of forty-two and one of his last acts was to ignore the established laws of primogeniture and declare that, not Pratap but his favourite son Jagmal will be his successor. The nobles and chiefs of Mewar however, knowing Pratap's great qualities of courage and leadership, considered this not only a great injustice but also inappropriate, as Jagmal was nowhere near Pratap's equal. The crowning ceremony was about to take place and Jagmal was moving to take possession of the throne and even while the trumpets were sounded and the heralds hailed him, the senior most of the noblemen, Krishna walked upto Jagmal, took his arm and gently but firmly removed him from the throne and placed him on another seat saying, 'Maharaj you have made a mistake, the throne belongs to your brother.' The nobles then went to the courtyard where Pratap was saddling for his departure. They led him back to the great hall and girding him with a sword, they seated him on the throne and hailed him the king of Mewar.

Soon after the ceremony was over, young Pratap remarked that ancient customs must not be forgotten, 'therefore to horse and slay a boar to Gouri'. He was referring to the custom of chivalry, which has been observed for centuries, known as the *teeka dour*. The custom says that soon after the prince has received the *teeka* of sovereignty, he at the head of his warriors makes a foray into the territory of anyone with whom he may have a feud; captures a stronghold or plunders a town and returns with the trophies. If however there is no quarrel with anyone and amity prevails all round, then a mock representation of the custom takes place or a hunt is ordered. In this case Pratap chose the last. They slew much game and the nobles looked forward to happier days for Mewar under the gallant Pratap.

Pratap was born in 1540 and ruled Mewar for twenty-five years from 1572 to 1597. He was now the king of the most distinguished and famous state of

*A mine explodes during the siege of Chittor*

Rajasthan. But the capital Chittorgarh had been lost to Emperor Akbar, his clans were demoralised after recent reverses and his financial resources were slender. Moreover Mewar was surrounded by the Mughal territory except in the south. Yet this indomitable Rajput was not deterred; his only aim in life was to recover Chittor and vindicate his honour. Pratap's task was made much more difficult by Akbar's clever policy. Although he had subjugated several Rajput princes, he soon healed the wounds he had inflicted and won over their loyalty by fair and honourable treatment and in some cases by ties of marriage. These rajas accepted alliances with the Empire and in return got important positions at the court and the *mansabs* (command of army units). In addition, Akbar wisely granted them much autonomy and did not interfere with their social, economic and religious life. Thus Maharana Pratap had ranged against him his kindred in faith and blood. The Rajput princes of Marwar, Amber, Bikaner and Bundi allied themselves with Akbar and became his sword arm. Even Pratap's own brothers Sagarji and Shakti Singh deserted him and joined the Mughals. Sagarji was rewarded for this treachery by Akbar and he was

*Fort of Chittor*

made the governor of Chittor. Thus Akbar had not only the huge resources of his empire behind him but also powerful allies. None of this deterred Rana Pratap and as the bard says; 'He swore to make his mother's milk resplendent,' and ultimately he did indeed amply redeem this pledge. For a quarter of a century Pratap fought single handed and withstood all the onslaughts of the mighty Mughals and their allies. A descendant of Bappa Rawal, he refused to bow his head to any mortal man. Akbar made several overtures and sent emissaries like Raja Maan Singh and Raja Todar Mal to Pratap, but to no avail.

*Maharana Pratap*

He went through terrible hardships and James Tod says, '...to recount them all, or relate the hardships he sustained would be difficult to believe and may even be pronounced a romance.' Pratap's main tactic at this stage was to raid the Mughal territory, cause much destruction and quickly retire into the safety of the mountains. His family had to hide in forests and survive on wild grain and fruits. Many a time he entrusted their care to tribes of the forest.

His noble vassals supported him devotedly with men and arms. Wealth and fortune were dangled as baits by the enemy but not one of his chieftains abandoned Pratap. The sons of Jaimal, the hero of the siege of Chittor, shed their blood as did the famous Chandrawats of Salumber and the brave chief of Dailwara. These and many other chiefs vied with each other, to hold aloft the 'standard of the sun' and fight and die along with Pratap.

To keep alive the memory of the desolation of Chittor, Pratap gave up the use of every article of luxury until Chittor was recovered and Mewar's honour restored.

The gold and silver dishes used by the royalty for dining were put aside and instead food was served on a *patera* of leaves. Comfortable beds were given up and were substituted by straw to sleep on and the beards were left uncut. He also ordered that the giant *nakkaras* (war drums) which were always sounded in the van of battle or processions should follow in the rear. All these traditions were maintained till recent years by Pratap's successors, but with a convenient amendment, they ate off gold and silver but placed leaves under the dishes; they slept on comfortable beds but placed straw under them!

Rana Pratap often used to say about his father, 'Had Udai Singh not intervened between him and his grandfather, the warrior Rana Sanga, no *Toork* would ever have given laws to Rajasthan.' It may also be added that this may have been so even if a less gifted sovereign than Akbar had been his adversary.

The first task Rana Pratap set himself was to improve the administration and governance of his government. His resources were limited therefore he had to exercise care in issuing new grants to his vassals and at the same time define the services that would be required. After the loss of Chittor, the stronghold of Kumbhalgarh was the new seat of government. This vast fort is located on a precipitous hill rising to 3,500 feet. Many other mountain forts like Gogunda were also strengthened.

Rana Pratap then resorted to the age old Mewar tactic and commanded his subjects to retire into the mountains. No cultivation or other activity was permitted in the plains. The fertile areas watered by the two rivers were rendered barren and grass grew on the fields instead of corn. This destructive policy of laying waste the resources of their own country and attacking the enemy forces as opportunity offered had persisted from the tenth century onward. Thus the whole area was of no value to the Mughals. The roads were rendered impassable by Pratap's men who often came down from the Aravalli mountains and having devastated whatever was of value to the enemy withdrew to the intricate ravines baffling all pursuit. The commerce which had been established between the Mughals and Europe and which went through Surat and other parts was intercepted and plundered. Communication and trade had to be abandoned.

Akbar finally invaded Mewar and established his headquarters at Ajmer. As mentioned, Akbar had close ties with many Rajput kings. He had married princesses from both Amber and Marwar. These and other chiefs had received much wealth and land for becoming satraps. Pratap had nothing but disdain for his brother princes who had thus degraded themselves. He foreswore any matrimonial alliances or other relationships with them. However, in their heart of hearts, these princes had a nagging respect for Pratap and could not help a sense of inferiority.

Raja Maan Singh of Amber who had given his sister in marriage to Akbar was one of the most important generals of the empire. He had conducted brilliant campaigns from Kabul to Bengal and beyond with a Rajput army and Akbar felt greatly beholden to him. Raja Maan Singh was returning to the north after conquering some major towns on the southern fringes of the empire. En route he wished to visit Pratap at Kumbhalgarh and make yet another effort for an alliance with the Mughals. When Maan Singh arrived he was warmly received by Prince Amar Singh, the Rana's eldest son, and invited to sit down to a feast. Maan Singh enquired about Rana Pratap and the young prince had to make apologies for his absence, the reason for which was that he was indisposed. Maan Singh was outraged and leaving the food untouched he said, 'I have understood the reason for the Rana's indisposition.' As Maan Singh was mounting his horse, Pratap appeared and expressed his regret, but added, 'I will not eat with a Rajput who gave his sister to a *Toork*.' Maan Singh replied, 'Abide in peril then. If I do not humble your pride, my name is not Maan.' To which Pratap answered, 'I will always be happy to meet you on the battlefield.' One of Pratap's nobles added, in less dignified terms that Maan Singh should also bring along his *Phoopa* (uncle) Akbar. All this was reported to the emperor who was apprehensive of the revival of Hindu prejudice which he had hoped he had vanquished.

The result was the Battle of Haldighat fought in the intense heat of June 1576. The battle field is about 27 kilometres north of Udaipur and although the battle was lost, it has immortalised the name of Rana Pratap. There are many contemporary descriptions of the battle including Abul Fazl's *Akbarnama* and Al Badaun's eyewitness account as he took part in the battle. There are also Mewari chroniclers, notably, Nainsi, who have recorded Haldighat. The estimated numbers that fought on each side vary greatly from 80,000 in the Mughal army and Rana Pratap's 22,000 men to less than half these numbers. These figures could have been inflated but what is known is that Rana Pratap was outnumbered three or four to one. Thus he fought against all odds. The Mughal forces were led by the redoubtable Raja Maan Singh and among the commanders was Asaf Khan. Almost half the Mughal army was composed of Kachwaha Rajputs, Maan Singh's own clansmen, while the other half was Muslim troops. Both sides had war elephants that took an important part in the battle. Rana Pratap's army was not equipped with firearms while the Mughals had troops armed with muskets and swivelguns mounted on camels.

*Statue of Maharana Pratap commemorating the Battle of Haldighat*

Apart from Rajputs, Pratap's forces included the loyal aborigines, the Bhils armed with bows and arrows. At the order of the Rana, vast tracts of the countryside had been burnt and devastated, so that the Mughal troops could not depend on local supplies of food and fodder. Among his commanders was Ramdas, the son of Jaimal and also Hakim Khan Sur and his band of Afghan soldiers. Thus it was a mixed bunch with Hindus and Muslims on both sides. Abul Fazl noted that in the thick of battle it was difficult to distinguish between friend and foe! Pratap's other commanders included Maan Singh Jhala and his most important minister Bhama Shah with Pratap leading the centre.

Pratap staked all on a desperate frontal charge, he kept no disposable reserve nor rear guard for any emergency, indeed his total strength, being one-third or less of the Mughal numbers, was too small to permit him such a precaution without weakening his attacking columns and taking the momentum out of his attack. But for the rest of the battle I will rely on an abbreviated version of James Tod's dramatic account of it.

*Maharana Pratap's 'Coat of a thousand nails'*

The area is mountainous, forested and intricate to penetrate. The Haldighat plain is at the base of a mountain. Pratap posted 22,000 Rajputs on the cliffs overlooking the field of battle along with the faithful aborigines, the Bhils, armed with their natural weapon, the bow and arrow. Huge stones were placed to roll over the enemy.

At the pass, Pratap stood with the flower of Mewar and glorious was the struggle. Clan after clan emulated the daring of their prince who led the crimson banner into the hottest part of the field. In vain he strained every nerve to encounter Raja Maan; but though denied the luxury of revenge on his Rajput foe he made a good passage where Saleem seated on a war elephant, commanded his troops. The Mughal guards fell before Pratap but for the steel plates which defended Saleem's howdah (seat on an elephant) the lance of the Rajput would have deprived Akbar of his heir. His steed, the gallant Chetak, nobly seconded his lord and is represented in all historical drawings of this battle with one foot raised upon the elephant of the Mughal, while the rider has his lance propelled against the foe. The mahout was slain and the infuriated animal, now without control, carried off Saleem. On this spot the carnage was immense: the Mughals eager to defend Saleem, the heroes of Mewar to second their prince, who had already received seven wounds. Marked by the 'royal umbrella', which he would not lay aside and which collected the might of the army against him, Pratap was thrice rescued from amidst the foe and was at length almost overwhelmed, when the chief, Maan Singh Jhala gave a great instance of fidelity. He seized the insignia of Mewar and rearing the 'golden sun' over his own head, made good his way to an intricate position, drawing after him the brunt of the battle, while the prince was forced from the field. With all his brave vassals, the noble Jhala fell. Maan Singh Jhala's descendants are honoured in Mewar till this day. But this desperate valour was unavailing against such force with numerous field artillery and a dromedary corps mounting swivel guns. Of the 22,000 Rajputs assembled on that day at Haldighat only 8,000 left the field alive. Pratap ruling a modest sized state was fighting the greatest monarch in the world at the time.

Maan Singh Jhala's ploy enabled Pratap to leave the field, but he was alone and unattended. His horse, the gallant Chetak which had borne Pratap the whole day and in the thick of battle, was wounded on his foreleg. Despite this, Chetak carried Pratap to safety after leaping across a mountain stream. Legend has it that he was closely pursued by two Mughal chiefs who were gaining on Pratap. But Shakti Singh, Pratap's estranged brother, now fighting for the Mughals, also followed the Rana. Shakti Singh had become a traitor to Mewar, but seeing his brother flying unattended, a feeling of remorse and affection overcame him. He joined the pursuit but only to slay the two Mughal pursuers who fell beneath his lance, Shakti then begged forgiveness from his brother and they embraced each other. The faithful Chetak who had served

Pratap so faithfully for several years finally fell to the ground and as Pratap unbuckled his caparison he died. The Rana later raised a cenotaph to honour his horse and 'Chetak ka Chabootra' still stands near the village of Jharol. However, many present day historians feel that this stirring story of the meeting between the two brothers after the Battle of Halidighat is a legend penned in the seventeenth century in *Raj Prasthi* and has no historical basis.

Following the Mughal victory, Raja Maan Singh of Amber gave orders that Rana Pratap's army was not to be pursued. This is attributed to the fact that Maan Singh personally respected Pratap. However, soon afterwards the imperial forces occupied much of Mewar.

Meanwhile Pratap headed for Kumbhalgarh, the great fort deep in the Aravallis. The rains brought some respite, but later in the year, the Mughal forces appeared at Kumbhagarh. A gallant and protracted defence was made with the Mewaris holding out till the drinking water became infested with worms. The contamination of the Nogun Well was attributed to the Deora chief of Abu, who had defected to the enemy. The forts of Dhurmati and Gogunda also fell to Maan Singh and soon after the Mughals occupied Udaipur.

Pratap withdrew to Chavand in the heart of the mountainous territory of Chappan. From here he tried to establish links with other chiefs and rulers and create a loose federation against the Mughals. He encouraged the Raja of Idar to revolt against Akbar and had a hand in influencing Chandrasen of Marwar, who like Pratap had continued to resist Mughal domination. Pratap also got Rao Surtan of Sirohi and Taj Khan of Jalore to join him. Thereupon Akbar moved sternly against these allies and in due course the emperor managed to subdue them.

Meanwhile attempts by the imperial forces to trace Pratap in the mountains proved futile. Over the next few years, while he could not regroup his resources to take on the Mughal army in a pitched battle, he continued to take guerilla action on every available occasion. Imperial traffic along the Ajmer-Gujarat route was often disrupted. A 'scorched earth policy' was also adopted with crops destroyed and wells filled with earth and rubble to deter the Mughal occupying forces, along with constant attempts to sever their supply lines.

For nine years, between 1576 and 1585, there was constant warfare between Pratap and the Mughals. Mewar territory would be captured by them only to be retaken by Pratap, forcing the enemy to withdraw. But gradually Pratap was pushed back further and further into safer areas. His resources depleted steadily

while his misfortunes continued to rise. His family was a chief source of worry. Food was scarce and his beloved and precious wife was insecure in the cave. The only cradles for the royal children were baskets hung high in the trees to keep them safe from the wild animals. His chief dread was his family falling into enemy hands. On more than one occasion they had been saved by the faithful Bhils.

Akbar's spies reported on Pratap's travails and he was touched. Many at the court could not withhold their admiration. The Khan-e-Khanan Abdul Rahim wrote about Pratap, 'All is unstable in the world, land and wealth will disappear but the virtue of a great name lives forever. Patta (Pratap) abandoned wealth and land, and never bowed his head to man: alone, of all the princes of Hind, he preserved the honour of his race.'

The Mughals chased him ruthlessly and finally he was at the end of his tether. One day the sight of his children crying for food in the forest was just too much for him. He demanded terms from Akbar.

The Mughal court was delighted at this submission. Akbar announced public celebration. The Rajput chiefs congratulated the Emperor but in their heart of hearts they were downcast. Akbar showed Pratap's letter to Prithiraj, a prince of Bikaner, who was considered an adornment at Akbar's court. He had secretly hero worshipped Pratap and was filled with grief. He said, 'It is a forgery' and obtaining permission to verify the truth he wrote to the Rana saying, 'Our chiefs have lost their valour and our women their honour. Akbar has purchased

all, but Patta is beyond his price. Though Patta has squandered away wealth, yet this treasure he has preserved. Only the descendant of Hamir has been preserved from dishonour. What is the secret? None but the soul of manliness and his sword. With them he has retained Rajput pride.' It was a long letter and for Pratap it was equal to a whole army. It nerved him and roused him into action. He realised that eyes of his race were fixed upon him. He worked out a whole new strategy. He decided he would abandon Mewar and marching westward he would carve out a new kingdom of Sisodias on the banks of the Indus. He would reduce Mewar to a desert and leave nothing for his enemies. He got together all his chiefs and vassals and their men and all those who preferred exile to degradation. He descended from the mountains and had reached the western desert when an incident changed all his plans. Bhama Shah, his minister, whose ancestors had held this office for generations, came forward and in an act of devotion and loyalty to the Rana, placed before him all the accumulated wealth of several generations of his family estimated at rupees twenty-five lakhs and twenty thousand *mohars* (gold coins). This was a vast treasure and sufficient for the maintenance of an army of 25,000 men for twelve years. Mewar has

*The fortress of Kumbhalgarh*

preserved forever the name of Bhama Shah as her saviour. Rana Pratap immediately turned around, made his way back, collected more soldiers and reorganised his forces.

The Mughals knew of his abandoning Mewar and they imagined that he was well out of their domain. Pratap took them by total surprise. He attacked Dungarpur and Banswara and fell on Shahbaz Khan at Devar and cut his troops to pieces. The fugitives were pursued to Amet and Zaver, the governor of which shared the same fate. Before the Mughals could recover from their consternation, Kumbhalgarh was assaulted and taken and Abdulla and his garrison were put to the sword.

In 1580 Akbar appointed Abdul Rahim Khan-e-Khanan as the governor of Ajmer along with the charge of the campaign against Rana Pratap. But this did not stop Pratap. He went on to capture thirty-two fortified posts by surprise with the Mughal troops manning them being slaughtered. By 1583 western Mewar was back under his control.

Mughal pressure on Mewar had relaxed marginally by this time due to other internal crises which impinged on the emperor's attention. But in 1584-85 Akbar sent another expedition under Raja Jagannath Kachwaha with the task of capturing Pratap. But the Raja could not make much headway. This was the last expedition, in effect the last major campaign by the imperial forces against Rana Pratap. At this time Akbar had to move to Lahore in order to keep a better control over the north-west boundaries of his empire. Thereafter Akbar made no further military moves against Pratap.

Gradually ordinary people who had emigrated out of Mewar during the turbulent years of the Mughal-Mewar confrontation began to drift back to the land. Agricultural activity picked up, assisted by a series of good monsoon years. So did trade and economic activities.

In one short campaign of 1586, Pratap had recovered the whole of Mewar except Chittor and Ajmer, a tremendous feat against one of the greatest military powers of the world at the time. As an insult to Raja Maan Singh he invaded the latter's capital Amber and went on to sack the main commercial centre Malpura. The Mughals, who had occupied Udaipur, were also attacked and the city was regained by Pratap. It was a completely different situation to earlier years, this time the Mughals were abandoning territory with the Rajputs in pursuit. Despite his best efforts however, Pratap was never able to fulfill his ambition of recovering his ancestral capital Chittor, even though he managed to restore Mewar's control over some of the areas around Chittor.

During the later years of his life, Pratap enjoyed some tranquility. He had reigned for twenty-five years but his life had been one of constant struggle and deprivation. At one stage it had appeared hopeless to him but with great grit and determination he had regained most of his kingdom. But he worried about Mewar's future. His son Amar Singh was getting used to a life of ease. Would the modest dwellings of the royal family and the nobles give way to palaces and mansions? Would Prince Amar keep up the struggle for Mewar's independence? Would the blood they had shed be sacrificed to the love of ease and luxury? He shared his worries with his loyal nobles for some assurance that this country would not be abandoned to the *Toork*. The chiefs swore 'by the throne of Bappa Rawal' that they would not let any Maharana rest or indulge in luxury and build palaces until the whole of Mewar was recovered.

During his lifetime Pratap was adored by his people and admired by his enemies. Over the centuries, he would remain established in the popular mind and literature alike for the values he stood for and the qualities he represented.

Rana Pratap died in 1597 at the age of fifty-seven as a result of an internal injury suffered while out hunting. A cenotaph to him was raised at a nearby village of Bandoli. A Mughal historian wrote that when Pratap died an extraordinary thing happened: tears welled up Emperor Akbar's eyes and he wept.

4

# Three Great Princely States

My early education was at the Daly College in Indore. It was one of the four 'Chiefs Colleges' established by the British in the late 1800s for the princes of the Indian states. The objective was to transform the wayward and spoilt little boys into 'admirable young men' who could be effective props of British rule. The other three institutions were at Ajmer, Rajkot and Lahore for the royalty of their regions. Let me however hasten to add that I was a 'commoner', the first to be taken into the Daly College on merit while it was being transformed into a public school.

The school uniform still remained closed collar coats, breeches and turbans. The Daly College building, constructed in 1882, with its marble dome and *chattris* (domed pavilions) atop the towers, was more like a palace than a school. Oil paintings of maharajas in gilt frames adorned the walls of the great marble hall.

On annual prize giving day, one walked up stiffly in military style to the marble dais in the great hall to receive prizes in academia or sports. One year, as was usual, a maharaja was presiding over the function. When I shook his hand, while receiving a prize, I was astonished at how soft and clammy his hand was. I wondered how that hand could have held a sword.

Indore was one of the three major Maratha states along with Gwalior and Baroda, which were carved out by military adventurers at the point of the sword. They were tough, valiant warriors who led armies into battle. What had happened to them in three or four generations? The Revolt of 1857 was the point in history when the political emasculation of the Indian rulers began. Initially the British considered them potentially dangerous, but by the end of that century they had been softened and were perceived as bulwarks of the Indian empire. Provided total security from external aggression and even from internal uprising by their British masters, the princes, with some honourable exceptions, lost much of their earlier manliness and vigour; hence the soft clammy hands.

If you look back at the founders of the states of Indore, Gwalior and Baroda you wonder all the more. The great warrior Peshwa Baji Rao had identified two brilliant soldiers Malharrao Holkar and Ranoji Scindia who led his armies to many a victory. The third, Pilaji Gaekwad who established the state of Baroda, had initially opposed and fought against Baji Rao. It was only later that Baroda became a part of the Maratha confederacy.

Malharrao Holkar came from a humble background. His family belonged to the Dhangars or shepherd tribe also described as Gadarias. Malharrao's father was a cultivator in a village in the Deccan called Hull from which this chief and his descendants take their name 'Holkar'. Malharrao was born in about 1693, so he was five years older than Baji Rao. When Malharrao was only three or four years old, his father died and his mother, moved to the house of her brother who lived in Khandesh. It was there that young Holkar was brought up by his mother's brother, Bhojraj, who was in command of a section of irregular horses under a Maratha chief of rank.

*Malharrao Holkar*

According to a fable, and fables are commonly associated with the youth of several people who have attained eminence, one day when still a child, Malharrao went to sleep under the shade of a tree. As he slept, the sun moved and its rays fell upon the slumbering boy. When his mother came to fetch him, she saw an astonishing sight! A large cobra had expanded its hood and was shielding the child from the rays of the hot sun. At first she was alarmed but afterwards construing it favourably, she called her brother to see this strange sight and they both felt that it predicted the boy's future greatness. The pages of Indian folklore are full of serpents and this concept is not an extraordinary one. The earth itself is said to be resting on the thousand heads of a gigantic sea serpent! Soon after, Bhojraj had a vision of a goddess who told him that his nephew was destined to be a king. In due course, therefore, Bhojraj enlisted young Malharrao as a trooper. Whatever the circumstances which raised young Holkar from the occupation of a goatherd to that of a soldier, he soon showed that he was going to be a distinguished soldier. In one of the first actions in which he was engaged, he slew a leader belonging to Nizam-ul-Mulk's army. Malharrao's courage soon brought him rewards. Once, however, he nearly ended his career by striking Peshwa Balaji Vishwanath's son Baji Rao in the face because the latter had objected to Holkar cutting the peasant's corn to feed his horses. Baji Rao was generous enough to ask his father to spare the rough soldier. Holkar never forgot Baji Rao's generosity and served him faithfully and with distinction. Baji Rao was so pleased with him that he gave Holkar a command of 500 horses. After this, his progress to a high command was rapid. When Baji Rao successfully wrested large tracts from the Portuguese in the Konkan, Holkar was in the forefront of the action again and acquired much distinction. During the Peshwa's invasion of Malwa, he commanded the advance of the army. After Malwa was conquered, Holkar received his first lands in about 1732, which included large tracts north of the Narmada as well as the district of Indore.

Although he established his state in Central India, for the next thirty years, Malharrao's principal military achievements were in North India. 'His operations both alone and in combination with other chiefs extended from the province of Oudh to the Indus and from the hills of Rajputana to the mountains of Kumaon.' Holkar may be deemed, from the invasion of Malwa onwards to be the most distinguished of the military commanders of the Maratha Empire. He was always favoured by Baji Rao, and Holkar in return paid the Peshwa the greatest deference.

Major General Sir John Malcolm in his *A Memoir of Central India* published in the nineteenth century, relates the following incident which took place around 1751.

> The Vazier Sefdar Jung had, in the reign of Ahmed Shah, called in the Marathas to preserve Oude from the Rohillas and, during the war that ensued, Mulhar Row Holkar particularly distinguished himself, by the night attack he made with a very small body of troops. His success on this occasion has been ascribed to an ancient stratagem. He directed for torches and lights to be tied to the horns of several thousand cattle, which were driven in one direction, while in another he placed lights upon every bush and tree, and, when this was done, marched silently in the dark by a different route to the attack. The enemy, pressed in one quarter by an actual assault, and seeing lights in several others, thought themselves surrounded and in danger of destruction; they dispersed, and fled in dismay, leaving their camp to be plundered by the conquerors, whose leader acquired a just increase of fame from the victory; and, in recompense for his zeal and gallantry during the whole campaign, the Emperor granted him.... It is indeed stated, that when Mulhar Row Holkar was asked what rewards he wished, he replied that he was the officer of the Paishwah, and desired to have no country independent of him...

Other predatory warfare took Holkar into Rajasthan, where taking advantage of succession disputes among the Rajput states he extended Maratha revenue claims into that region. Next we see Malharrao in action in Punjab and beyond.

From ancient times the Punjab, unlike Rajasthan, had been easy prey and invaders had treated it more as a highway than a battleground. Ahmad Shah Abdali, the King of Afghanistan, after defeating the crumbling Mughals, conquered the Punjab in 1750. He needed the riches of this province as Afghanistan was a barren and poor country.

In January 1757, Abdali grew bolder. He arrived at Delhi and plundered the imperial city. He not only left his son Taimur Shah, as the viceroy of the Punjab, but also appointed a 'Supreme Agent' at Delhi to dictate to the Mughal Emperor. This, therefore, was the hopeless and woeful state of affairs in Hindustan.

*Maharaja Tukoji Rao Holkar of Indore, c. 1875, a descendant of Malharrao Holkar*

The Marathas had been watching the situation closely. In mid-1757, Raghunath Rao, Baji Rao's son, and that lion-hearted old soldier Malharrao Holkar, were given orders to attack Delhi. Holkar was now sixty-five years old but still leading his men into battle. The Afghan defence of Delhi proved futile against the combined attack of Raghunath and Holkar. The Afghans were expelled from the capital and the Mughal Emperor once again changed masters. Delhi was garrisoned by a strong Maratha force in exchange for tribute paid to them by the Mughals. The Marathas then redirected their efforts at reconquering the Punjab to save the people from the atrocities of the Afghan viceroy. They fell like a sudden calamity on the Afghans, and aided by bands of Sikhs, they captured Sirhind. Flushed with victory, Raghunath Rao and Holkar marched to Lahore. The Afghans could not defend the city and the Marathas entered Lahore in triumph in April 1758. Terror stricken and confused, Taimur Shah tried to organise a well-ordered retreat, but the Marathas were in such hot pursuit that the retreat became a rout. The Afghans abandoned much of the loot from Delhi, their equipment and even their artillery on the banks of the river Chenab. Several hundred Afghan and Uzbek soldiers who could not cross the flooded river were captured and brought back to Amritsar in chains. Raghunath Rao and Holkar, continuing the pursuit of the Afghans, captured Attock. The swallow-tailed standard was triumphantly raised on the ramparts of the fort accompanied by the thunder of the victorious Maratha cannons. The Deccan horses advanced to the river Indus and drank its waters, while the Maratha soldiers washed their blades and lances in the river. Then ordered by Malharrao Holkar, Tukoji Holkar penetrated into Peshawar and the

*Chhatri of Malharrao Holkar at Alampaur*

Khyber Pass. A second Maratha force entered Multan and crossing the Indus, occupied Dera Ghazi Khan and its neighbourhood.

These were indeed the years of Maratha glory and the zenith of their power. Their right to tribute was acknowledged on the banks of the lower Kaveri in Tamil Nadu and the Deccan horse had reached the Indus.

These years however were short-lived. In 1761, Abdali was back and the battle of Panipat was lost. Before this battle Holkar had, for sound military reasons, entreated his commander Sadesheo Bhau to delay the action for one or two days, but the latter whose pride and vanity were great, impatient of the advice exclaimed, 'Who wants the counsel of a goatherd?' The incensed Holkar withdrew his troops during the early stage of this battle. This, of course, later gave rise to severe reproaches as the battle was of crucial importance to the nation. A similar taunt by Sadesheo Bhau lost the Maratha commander the services of one of his most efficient allies, Suraj Mal, the Jat prince of Bharatpur.

When Malharrao died at the age of seventy-six, he left behind for his family large domains in Central India, the Deccan, Khandesh, as well as in four districts in Rajasthan. He had for more than forty years of his life been a commander of reputation and one of the most distinguished in the Maratha confederacy. He was a man of simple manners and manly courage. He personally had no regard for money and was generous to a fault. Whenever he was pleased with a soldier's gallantry he would exclaim, 'Fill his shield with money!' He was always willing to lend money to friends although he knew it would be returned but rarely. Malharrao also had a mischievous sense of humour and on Baji Rao's invasion of Delhi, Holkar to show his contempt for the Emperor, had a hog strung up on one of the outer gates of Delhi. Baji Rao reprimanded him royally for the prank.

According to Kincaid and Parasnis, 'Ranoji Scindia came from an ancient Kshatriya family of which the original name was Sendrak.' But Major General Sir John Malcolm

*Maharaja of Gwalior with Sardars, 1882*

says in his authoritative *A Memoir of Central India*, 'The family of Sindia is Sudras of the tribe of Koombee or cultivators.' Whatever the origin Kshatriya or Sudra—the Scindias rose to considerable eminence. One of Ranoji's descendants was an extraordinary man, Mahadji Scindia, who extended his authority over North India and made the helpless and confused Mughal Emperor Shah Alam II, his puppet. At the time of Partition, the great princely state of Gwalior was among the five largest in India.

Ranoji Scindia, the first who achieved distinction as a soldier, succeeded his father as *patel* (village headman) of a village near Wye. Later he was in the service of Balaji Vishwanath, after whose death he continued in that of his son, Baji Rao. The humble employment of Ranoji Scindia was to carry the Peshwa's slippers. What influenced the *patel* of a village to accept this menial service? It was probably not indigence but ambition as subsequent events proved. Luck was also on Ranoji's side. One day, Baji Rao was in a long audience with King Shahu. When he came out he found Ranoji in deep slumber, but still clasping to his chest the Peshwa's slippers. Baji Rao was impressed, believing that one who was so faithful in small things would prove no less faithful in great ones. Baji Rao promptly appointed Ranoji to the *pagah* (bodyguard).

From then on his rise was rapid and when Baji Rao invaded Malwa, Ranoji was fighting in the first rank of the Maratha chiefs.

John Malcolm states that this anecdote about the slippers is corroborated by a letter of Captain Steward (Acting Resident at Scindia's court) dated 3 September 1819: 'Ranoji (he observes) is stated, after he was promoted, to have carried with him carefully packed in a box, a pair of the Paishwah's old slippers, which he never ceased to regard with almost religious veneration as the source of his rise.'

Ranoji appears to have been a splendid soldier and leader. He was reportedly very extravagant and his expenses always exceeded his income. When broke, he usually asked his good friend Malharrao Holkar for a loan and the latter, always generous, never demurred. It was not often that Ranoji repaid the loan he had received!

Emperor Aurangzeb had once described Gujarat as the beauty and ornament of India. Through Surat passed the enormous volume of Muslim pilgrims to the holy cities of Arabia. Travellers, merchants, fortune hunters and political refugees from Persia, Arabia, Turkey, Zanzibar and even Khurasan and Barbary used to enter India through the Gujarat ports.

Gujarat had for decades been the battleground for the Marathas and the Mughals, with the Marathas plundering the rich cities and emptying the treasuries and the Mughals on the defensive trying to stem the raids.

About the year 1725, Hamid Khan, the governor of Gujarat rebelled against his Mughal masters. The debauched Emperor Mohammad Shah had to order Rustam Ali Khan, the Mughal governor of neighbouring Surat to subdue him. Rustam Ali's armies not being strong enough to do so, he sought the assistance of a Maratha chieftain Pilaji Gaekwad. Thus we have the Surat Governor Rustam Ali and Pilaji Gaekwad ranged against the rebel Hamid Khan.

Pilaji Gaekwad needs the spotlight for a while as he was the founder of the great state of Baroda. We have written about Scindia of Gwalior and Holkar of Indore.

These, along with Gaekwad of Vadodara, were some of the major Maratha states established at this time. The name Gaekwad is wrongly interpreted to mean 'cowherd'. According to the Pilaji Gaekwad *bakhar* (chronicle), an ancestor of Pilaji named Nandaji was in charge of Bher Fort. One day, a Muslim butcher drove a herd of cows past the fort gates obviously intending to slaughter them for beef. Nandaji's Hindu susceptibilities were outraged and he stopped the herd and drove the cows into the fort through a *kawad* (side door). In Marathi or Hindi the word *gai* means cow and *kawad*, a small door, Gaekwad is therefore a cow's door, which was the name given to Nandaji after his virtuous feat.

Nandaji's great-grandson Pilaji Gaekwad had the position of a horse-master in the household of Dabhade, the commander-in-chief of the Maratha army. Some forty or fifty horses, which had become too thin to carry Dabhade's troopers, were put in Pilaji's charge. Shortly afterwards, the horses came back in excellent condition.

*Laxmi Vilas Palace of the Gaekwads at Baroda, built in the late 1870s*

Dabhade then gave him 300 other foundered horses which also recovered their health and strength. Not only did Pilaji send them back in first rate condition but he also returned a part of the money given to him for their keep. As a reward, Dabhade promoted Pilaji to the command of two squadrons and allowed him to establish himself at a fort near Surat to which Pilaji gave the name Songadh or the Golden Fort. After this bit of fortune, Pilaji went from strength to strength and became the head of an important army formation.

As mentioned earlier Pilaji Gaekwad had agreed to join the Mughal general Rustam Ali, against Hamid Khan, the rebel governor of Gujarat. An indecisive action was fought between the adversaries. Hamid Khan, unsure of his strength, then decided to use intrigue as his weapon. He induced some Maratha Sardars, who were his allies to win over their fellow Maratha, Pilaji Gaekwad, from the Mughal general Rustam Ali's side. When the battle resumed, Pilaji who had secretly switched loyalties, cleverly obtained leave from his commander Rustam Ali, to guard the guns and baggage, while Rustam Ali charged the enemy. Away went the glittering masses

*King of Baroda on a great sowari*

of imperial Mughal horses, with standards flying and lances glinting. Pilaji Gaekwad instantly spiked his commander's guns and gave the order to his cavalry to charge right into the rear! If ever a cavalry leader had a problem, it was Rustam Ali. He, poor man, was attacked from the front by Hamid Khan, the rebel and in the rear by Pilaji. Rustam Ali's Mughal force was destroyed and the over-trusting general fell on the battlefield. The grateful Hamid Khan granted the *chauth* (one-fourth of the revenue) of Gujarat to Pilaji and returned in triumph to Ahmedabad. However, his stay there was not for long.

The defeat of Rustam Ali was a calamity for the Delhi government and a setback for the imperial authority. Sarbuland Khan, the erstwhile governor of Kabul was next ordered to go forthwith to Gujarat with reinforcements and drive out Hamid Khan and Pilaji Gaekwad. Sarbuland managed to force his way to Ahmedabad, the capital, but was powerless to restore order. While Hamid Khan fled to the Deccan to join the Nizam, Pilaji Gaekwad continued his depredations. Sarbuland was unable to control him and was forced to give him drafts for large amounts of money on the chief bankers of Gujarat. On the basis of these drafts issued by the governor, the Maratha leader extorted vast sums of money from the wealthy men of the province, resulting in much trade and capital fleeing from Gujarat.

Sarbuland Khan, already discredited at court, received no further help from Delhi and was unable to curb the activities of Pilaji and his Maratha forces. Soon he advanced further and occupied Baroda and Champaner, thus getting nearer to the centre of the province. After various twists of fortune, Pilaji succeeded in establishing the state of Baroda.

5

# Random Images of the Revolt of 1857~58

My great-grandfather Subedar Major Ranveer Singh fought in the Great Revolt. Unfortunately he fought on the wrong side and thereby hangs a tale which will follow later.

It is not often realised that the Revolt of 1857-58 was the biggest and the bloodiest conflict against any European colonial power in the nineteenth century. It involved over 200,000 soldiers on both sides as well as innumerable Indian civilians and peasants who picked up their swords and muskets to fight the British. The fighting went on for almost two years and mutual hatred led to unbelievable atrocities. This was a revolt against one of the greatest empires of the recent times. The sun never set on the British empire because it has been said, even God, did not trust them in the dark.

It started as a one man rebellion on 29 March 1857. Lieutenant Baugh arrived at the lines in Barrackpore near Calcutta, and saw a single *sipahi* (anglicised to sepoy) marching up and down in front of the guard comprising twenty men, exhorting them to join him and strike a blow for their religion. 'Come out you *behnchuds* (seducers of your sisters) why are you not joining me? You are the ones who incited me to do this. Get ready you rascals.' He also threatened to shoot the first white man he saw. It was no idle threat, for as soon as the *sipahi* saw Lieutenant Baugh, he fired. The shot missed Baugh but brought his horse down. The lieutenant also fired, but missed. Then began a desperate hand to hand encounter. The *sipahi* drew his sword, there was an arcing flash of steel and Baugh was desperately clutching his bloodied arm. Sergeant Hewson rushed to his help, but the *sipahi* was a better swordsman than both and wounded not only Baugh but also the sergeant. The guard of twenty *sipahis* stood stock still and watched the *firangees* (foreigners) fighting for their lives. The sergeant shouted for help; only one man from the guard, Sheikh Paltu came forward. He crept up behind the fighting *sipahi* and held him from the back. The two white soldiers ran for their lives. The *sipahi* then taunted his comrades for letting him fight alone. Meanwhile other European officers rushed

*The attack of mutineers, July 30, 1857*

to the scene. Brigadier Grant drew his revolver and told the guard, 'The first man who refuses to obey the order is a dead man.' Sullenly the guard moved forward. When the lone rebel saw the day was lost, he turned the musket upon himself. He was wounded but unfortunately could not save himself from a felon's death. The *sipahi*, Mangal Pandey was twenty-six years old. Soon the cry 'Remember Mangal Pandey' was to become a signal of revolt.

The Mutiny, the Great Revolt or Rebellion, the National Uprising or the War of Independence—call it what you will, the scholars are still arguing about it. Maharaja Scindia of Gwalior, the Nizam of Hyderabad, and the states of the Punjab, the Sikh *sipahis* as well as some Punjabi Muslims and Pathans came to the assistance of the beleaguered British. The Sikhs in particular, long hostile to the Mughal rule, and lately defeated in the Sikh Wars by the now mutinous *Purabias* (people from eastern Uttar Pradesh) of the Bengal army, promptly gravitated to the British. The Raja of Jind even offered to personally lead his troops against the rebels. Had it not been for these, the story of 1857-58 might well have been different.

In addition, the Begum of Bhopal, Gulab Singh of Kashmir, the Maharaja of Jodhpur and importantly Jang Bahadur of Nepal, with a strong Gurkha army, rendered invaluable help to the enemy. All the people mentioned in the last two paragraphs consigned us to ninety years more of slavery.

Interestingly, while the Maharaja of Gwalior stuck with the British, his well-trained army at a later stage joined the Rani of Jhansi and fought against the imperialists. In the case of Jodhpur also, while the Maharaja immediately offered to help his masters, the Jodhpur Legion deserted to the rebels.

The areas south of the river Narmada did not join the Revolt. The armies of the Madras and Bombay Presidencies remained loyal to their foreign masters and helped restore order at a later stage. Thus it was mainly *Arya-varta* (the Aryan homeland) that rose in revolt.

In most accounts, the greased cartridge has been referred to as the spark and tinder that lit the flames of rebellion. Disraeli said in the Parliament, 'Revolutions are not made of grease,' implying that there were many other underlying causes which we will not get into here.

An interesting sidelight during the Revolt was the appearance of the mysterious 'chapattis'. It was reported that four chapattis would be sent to the watchmen of four neighbouring villages and each village in turn had been told to send four other chapattis to four other villages and so on. Thus the distribution of chapattis increased in geometric progression. By this means the chapattis were travelling all over Hindustan at the rate of 150 kilometres in twenty-four hours. The newspapers in Delhi were full of this phenomenon. It was also being said that an ominous slogan '*Sab lal hogaya hai*' (Everything is becoming red) was being whispered everywhere. It was never understood what the exact significance of these curious chapattis or 'puris' was. Many thought them signalling that dramatic upheavals were about to take place across Hindustan. It was also said that upon the earlier downfall of the Maratha

*Disarming the 11th Irregular Cavalry at Berhampore during the 1857 Rebellion*

power, a piece of bread had passed from village to village. Thus it was now signalling the collapse of British power.

Although we started with the one man rebellion of Mangal Pandey, he was almost irrelevant to the Mutiny. The actual Revolt started almost a month and a half later at Meerut, an important military station. Eighty-five *sipahis*, repulsed at the idea of biting the greased cartridges, refused to do so and were court-marshalled. The commander at Meerut was General Hewitt, sixty-seven years, old, extremely fat and totally lazy. A colleague described him as 'a fearful old dolt ... An exasperating idiot'. This man rejected a plea for mercy against the ten years rigorous imprisonment imposed on these eighty-five men, who had refused to bite the cartridges, and even suggested the death sentence for some of them.

The sentenced *sipahis* were assembled in front of the cantonment troops, the white soldiers with their guns loaded and sabers drawn. The *sipahis*, some with several years of honourable service behind them, were stripped of their uniforms, their boots removed and their ankles shackled. When they were marched off, they threw their boots at the colonel and cursed loudly in Hindustani, '*In lal moo kay bandroon se badla!*' (Revenge against these red faced monkeys!) These were proud men who had fought for the British in many campaigns and never wavered in their allegiance.

A day after the public humiliation of these brave soldiers, on 10 May 1857 their comrades-in-arms at Meerut rose as one, to free them. They broke open the armoury and rampaged through the cantonment, massacred the Europeans and set their bungalows on fire. Interestingly there were as many British as Indian troops in the station and more importantly the British had the artillery, yet there was no resistance organised by them. The military authorities were paralysed.

Even stranger was that British intelligence was so poor that they had no idea of the coming catastrophe. Till the weather permitted, cricket matches were being played, and in the cantonment the ritual of balls and racing was being enjoyed.

Having slaughtered most of the foreigners in sight, the *sipahis* rode 64 kilometres to Delhi, galloped across the bridge of boats that spanned the river

*Bahadur Shah Zafar: The last Mughal*

Yamuna and entered the capital. They then went to the Red Fort and called upon Bahadur Shah Zafar to assume command. He was eighty-two years old and had been on the throne for twenty years, but he was a king without a kingdom, 'a chessboard king'. Although he was still revered by the common man in the street as the lineal successor of Akbar and Shah Jahan, he was a puppet of the British and his authority lay within the confines of the Red Fort. The *sipahis* galloped into the open air audience hall of the fort with swords drawn and demanded that he take over as the rightful emperor. Bahadur Shah pleaded old age and infirmity, he pleaded poverty, but the rebels would not be denied. They had come to resurrect the Mughal Empire and fight for both Hinduism and Islam. And so this broken old man was hailed as the Emperor of Hindustan. The proclamation was accompanied by booming cannons and the news went around that the British Raj had ended.

Five months later, the British reoccupied the capital and Delhi suffered its reign of terror. Bahadur Shah was banished to Rangoon (Yangon) where he died a few years later, far from home and family, unhonoured and unsung. His grave, which I visited on a recent tour to Yangon, is located in the centre of the town. It is a simple grave with no embellishment and is under a shed type of structure surrounded by a small garden.

The struggle was marked by merciless killing and many innocent men, women and children were slaughtered on both sides. One of the most gruesome

Public hanging of two rebels during the Revolt

punishments adopted by the British was the blowing away of rebels from the mouth of cannons. The victim was lashed to a cannon, the small of his back or the pit of his stomach against the muzzle and then, he was smeared with the blood of the Englishman killed by the rebels. When the gun was fired, the head of the victim, hardly disfigured, would fly through the smoke and then fall to the ground slightly blackened, followed by the arms and legs, which would also be only partially mutilated. The trunk would, of course, be shattered and pieces of flesh and intestines and blood would fall on the gunners and the eager spectators who had ventured too close. The vultures flying above would, with amazing skill, snap up bits of flesh in their beaks.

While British historians have described in grisly detail the atrocities of the Indians, they have, with a few honourable exceptions, glossed over the horrors perpetuated by their own countrymen. Throwing away their mask of civilisation the British engaged in such savagery that, as one English writer put it, 'a reasonable parallel can be seen in our own times with the Nazi occupation of Europe.'

One of the places where the insurrection broke out was Nasirabad in Rajasthan (about 20 kilometres from Ajmer). Many men here remained true to their English officers, but still did not act against the rebels either. My great-grandfather was a Subedar Major in the Rajputana Infantry as the Rajputana Rifles were then called, because at the time they were not equipped with rifles. Subedar Major was the highest rank an Indian could attain. There was only one Subedar Major per regiment, while there were ten subedars. The pay of an ordinary *sipahi* was Rs. 7 per month but as it cost only Rs. 2 to put up a hut of bamboo, matting and mud for his wife and children at the military station, it seems to be ample. Subedar Majors must have been paid a more handsome wage of Rs. 30 to Rs. 35 per month. An early photograph shows Ranveer Singh as a tall, strong man. This leads to an interesting point regarding the physique of *sipahis* at this time.

Hibbert in *The Great Mutiny* writes, 'The sepoys were also of more imposing physique than European soldiers since there was never a shortage of recruits, and commanding officers were able to choose only the strongest, tallest and most presentable-looking men. In the Bengal Army most soldiers, both Muslim and Hindu, were enlisted in Oudh, whose capital was Lucknow. They were generally taller than the white soldiers, few being less than five feet eight inches. Three out of four

*The Sikander Bagh in Lucknow was the venue of a fierce battle during the 1857 uprising*

*A group of sepoys at Lucknow*

were Hindus, and these most were high-caste Brahmins or Rajputs, the profession of arms being considered by Hindus worthy and honourable ...'

Unfortunately, and as I explain later, understandably, Ranveer Singh remained 'true to his salt' and when Nasirabad erupted, he did not join the rebels but fought on the wrong side. Why did Subedar Major Ranveer Singh not mutiny? I am elaborating on this as it illustrates one of the main causes of the Revolt. In the early 1800s or several decades before the Revolt, there was a close bond between the white officers and the *sipahis*. Sita Ram Pande, who was a subedar and had fought for the British in Afghanistan, is quoted by historians as saying, 'I was good friends with the English soldiery and in the old days they used to treat the sepoy with great kindness. At that time many European officers knew our language pretty well ... They mixed more with us. The sahib often used to give "nautches" for the regiment and they attended our games.' But by the time of the Revolt, all this had changed. As the

British spread their tentacles over the country they became more arrogant. There was no fellow feeling between the white minority and the Indians in the army and the good understanding that had prevailed in the early days of the Company had become a thing of the past. An English officer is quoted, 'The sepoy is esteemed as an inferior creature. He is sworn at. He is spoken of as a "nigger" and addressed as a *suar* or pig.' With the loss of goodwill, discipline in the army also suffered heavily.

What has all this got to do with Ranveer Singh? Some British officers had not changed and still kept a close relationship and understanding with their men. Such a man was Colonel or Captain Drynan of the Rajputana Infantry which was Ranveer Singh's unit. Drynan had a Swiss wife whose language was French. They had no children. The Drynans, husband and wife, became very fond of Ranveer Singh's pretty little daughter oddly named Phepli, educated her and literally brought her up. So my grandmother, a village girl from Rajasthan, grew up speaking French! How could the Subedar Major have rebelled? Had the close relations between the English officers and Indian *sipahis* continued as in the past it may have been much more difficult for the *sipahis* to rebel and slaughter their officers. But arrogance begets hatred and respect begets fellow feeling.

Though the Revolt failed in its objective, even in failure it served a grand purpose. It was a source of inspiration for the national liberation movement, which later achieved what the Revolt could not.

6

# The Women of Bhopal

My nana (maternal grandfather) arrived in Bhopal around 1902 as a young doctor. He had qualified as an LMP which stood for Licentiate Medical Practitioner. I am sure that modern day doctors have never heard of an LMP! One evening as he was cycling back from the hospital along the shores of the lake, he spotted a few boys swimming some distance from the shore. He suddenly realised that two were in serious trouble as they were entangled in the weeds. A powerful swimmer, my grandfather peeled off his sherwani and his pump shoes and leapt into the water. He managed to pull out the two exhausted lads and to his utter surprise one of them turned out to be a prince. The Begum of Bhopal at the time was the matronly Sultan Jahan and it was her son who had been rescued. She took a motherly interest in the young doctor and not many years later he was the proud owner of a *jagir* (estate) consisting of several villages. The pious, upright Sultan Jahan was the last of the many begums of Bhopal.

Bhopal was known for two things; one, its beautiful lake and landscape and two, some remarkable women who had ruled there. The lake lies between two hills and is huge, measuring almost 14 kilometres in length. It was created by a dam across the river Banganga almost 300 years ago. The second noteworthy aspect is the line of the seven extraordinary women who played a major role in its history. These seven women dominated the principality for 160 years out of Bhopal's 240 year history. One hears of the four famous begums of Bhopal who ruled the state. What is less well known is that before them, there were three other women who guided the destiny of the state. Strangely all three were Hindu women, two of whom married the then nawabs.

The rule of the women started in the early 1700s with Kamlapati, who was the Rani of the Gond tribe in the region. Next was Fateh Bibi, the Rajput wife of the founder of Bhopal, Dost Mohammad Khan. The third important woman was the Brahmin Dowager Mamola Bai, who married the fourth Nawab of Bhopal and after his early death, governed in the name of her weak and ineffectual stepsons for fifty years. After her came four extraordinary women who reigned as begums over the state for more than a century from 1819 to 1926.

Bhopal in Central India was among the leading princely states in India with a 19 gun salute, which was only granted to ten other major states in the country. It was the second largest Muslim state after Hyderabad and had a Hindu population of 90 per cent.

The state was founded by a Pathan mercenary who came from the Afghan frontier. He had joined the Mughal army and was posted in Malwa. In the chaos following Aurangzeb's death, Dost Mohammad found himself surrounded by Rajput and Maratha

warlords jostling for power. He took on lease a village called Berasia and used it as a military base. He and his band attached themselves as mercenaries to various local warlords. With a mixture of daring and abysmal treachery he grew in strength.

At this time, the territory around the lake of Bhopal was under the control of a Gond warlord. The Gonds and Bhils are the indigenous tribes of Central India. This Gond Raja took as his wife Kamlapati, a woman of luminous beauty. Claudia Preckel in her book on Bhopal quotes an Urdu writer who describes Kamlapati as having, 'Such fine translucent skin, that betel juice when being swallowed would trace her neck with a pink flush.' It is not clear whether Kamlapati was a Gond herself or belonged to some other ethnic group.

Her husband, the Gond Raja was one of the most powerful chieftains of the area. He captured the strong fort of Ginnor and built a seven-storey palace for Kamlapati on the shores of the Bhopal Lake, which stands to this day. It is said that the Raja's supremacy over the other warlords was largely due to the wisdom and farsightedness of his rani. Unfortunately a young relative of her husband became obsessed by the beauty of Kamlapati. He declared his feelings for her but was rejected outright. Undeterred he continued to make advances and not being able to gain her by fair means, he invited the Raja to a Gond feast, at which the latter was poisoned and killed.

The rani was thus left a widow at the mercy of this dangerous blackguard. Feeling totally vulnerable, despite the love her people had for her, she looked for protection. Dost Mohammad and his kinsman were known mercenaries in the area and she sought his protection offering him a lakh of rupees. As soon as Dost Mohammad accepted the offer, the clever woman tied a *rakhi* (bracelet) which made Dost her *rakhi* brother and so precluded possible lustful advances. Dost Mohammad faithfully discharged his duties and gave full protection to the rani and she ruled successfully over her Gond domain for over a decade.

*Dost Mohammad Khan*

When Kamlapati died in 1723, the protector became a predator. He grabbed her palace and jewels and in due course he took over her whole kingdom. Dost then went back to Afghanistan in order to recruit more of his kinsmen for his army in Bhopal. While Dost was away, his young wife Fateh Bibi was in charge of his domain. She is the second woman to have played a major role in the affairs of Bhopal. Fateh Bibi, it is said, was a Rajput girl from Mangalgarh, which was a small principality of Malwa. Fateh Bibi was a devoted wife and a courageous companion of Dost Mohammad. She accompanied her husband on his wanderings and even on some of his skirmishes on horseback. Doing that, veiled from head to toe in a burqa, along with a large band of marauders, would not have been easy. She had also financed the lease of her husband's first military outpost of Berasia, from where he started his career as a mercenary.

When Dost returned to Afghanistan to raise fresh recruits, Fateh Bibi literally held the fort in his absence. In those turbulent times the Rajput and Maratha predatory bands roamed the Malwa plateau. She fended off many attacks on Dost Mohammad's stronghold and it is on account of Fateh Bibi that her husband found his territory intact when he returned from Afghanistan. He now had an army of 10,000 men and built a fort near the lake, which he named Fatehgarh after his wife Fateh Bibi. Even the flag of Bhopal was called 'Fateh nishan'. Abida Sultan, the last heir apparent of Bhopal, commented on this dedication, 'An extraordinary tribute, coming as it did 300 years ago from an Oriental male'. By now Bhopal state was firmly established on the map of Central India.

After Dost Mohammad's death in 1740, there was a struggle for succession but with the help of the Nizam of Hyderabad, Dost's son Yar Mohammad succeeded to the throne. Yar however did not possess his father's abilities. He was defeated by the Marathas several times and was forced to pay tribute to them.

Yar Mohammad married a beautiful and talented woman named Mamola Bai whose origins are not recorded. It is however known that she was a Hindu and probably a Brahmin. She was another woman who dominated the affairs of Bhopal state. Yar was a weak ruler and even during his lifetime, Mamola was very powerful at his court. Yar died young and there was a struggle for succession, but his wife put down the various claimants to the throne, one by one, through armed action and became the de facto ruler.

Another relative, Sharif Mohammad made a bid for power and attacked Bhopal in February 1787. Mamola Bai sent a strong force against him and in a battle near a village called Phanda, Sharif and six of his brothers were killed. It was Mamola who thus demonstrated to the people of Bhopal that a woman could rule as effectively as any male. Abida Sultan says in her book, 'At this time Mamola began to be called Maiji Sahiba (Madam Mother) and was revered for her piety, wisdom and skill in consolidating and retaining the state during a particularly turbulent period.'

In later years, Bhopal state became close to the British East India Company and this is what ensured its survival. Mamola adept at state craft was the first ruler to befriend the British. Four thousand of their troops in the area under Colonel Goddard were beleaguered by the Marathas and would have been decimated but for the hand of friendship extended by Mamola. This stood Bhopal in good stead in later years.

In his account published in 1884, Major William Hough writes of Mamola. 'The history of this extraordinary princess, ... who for more than half a century greatly influenced, the councils of Bhopal, if she did no control, is very extraordinary ... she came from Upper Hindustan. ... She had herself no children ... She was beloved and respected by all. Her memory is still cherished by the natives, both Hindu and Mahomedan, of Bhopal.'

Mamola Bai died in 1792 at the ripe old age of eighty. After her death, the fortunes of Bhopal were at their lowest ebb. Daulat Rao Scindia invaded the state and taking control appointed an administrator. The continued harassment by the Marathas finally drove Bhopal into the arms of the British and a treaty was signed in 1818 according to which the then nawab accepted the suzerainty of the East India Company in return for Bhopal's security. This treaty ensured the territorial integrity of the state against the aggressive Marathas. Without this treaty Bhopal in fact, may not have survived as a state.

*Qudsiya Begum, the first Begum of Bhopal*

Thus in 1818, we come to the 'great century of women's rule in Bhopal'. The then Nawab Nazar Mohammad died suddenly at the age of twenty-eight years, not without suspicion of his being poisoned. His widow Qudsiya was just seventeen years old and was installed by the British as the ruler of Bhopal. She thus became the first of the four Begums of Bhopal and ruled for nineteen years from 1818 to 1837.

There were many male aspirants to the throne, but she set aside their claims on the grounds that the only rightful ruler was her one-year-old daughter. Some rivals she bought over by granting them lucrative *jagirs*, while with others she struck shrewd deals. As regards the principal contender to the throne Amir Khan, Qudsiya agreed to betroth her infant daughter Sikandar to his eldest son Munir, so that he could on marriage take over as the nawab. Having neatly organised all this, Qudsiya boldly declared herself as regent until Sikandar, her daughter, reached the age of maturity. She could then look forward to sixteen years as ruler of Bhopal.

Qudsiya was a tall, thin, plain woman. She was completely illiterate but blessed with political acumen. She had strictly observed purdah since her youth. But when she took over as regent, in a bold move, unheard of at the time, she threw away the veil as she felt that she could not be an effective ruler shrouded from head to toe in a burqa.

Having overcome the immediate crisis of rival contenders, her object then was to demonstrate her power to her numerous enemies. She attended military exercises, learnt the art of war and displayed her ability to use weapons, ride horses and elephants. She was successful in convincing her nobles and her subjects that she was the right person to rule the state in those days of war and political instability.

During her years as regent, Qudsiya was supported by Balthazar de Bourbon or Shahzad Masih as he was called in Bhopal. 'There was a deep bond of friendship, perhaps of affection between them.' In fact there is a suggestion that Qudsiya and Balthazar de Bourbon were lovers. He successfully led some military actions in support of her. Several years later he was poisoned by some Afghan nobles.

The ancestors of the Bhopal Bourbons were originally from France and were connected to the royal family of Bourbons. According to their family annals, the first Bourbon to come to India had to flee France after he had killed a rival in a duel. The family, after much wandering, appeared in Bhopal around 1783, and became leading figures at the court. However, during the reign of subsequent Begums they lost their importance. Their descendants still live in Bhopal.

*Moti Masjid*

Shaharyar Khan, a direct descendant of Qudsiya, has written a fascinating account of the Begums of Bhopal. He would have been the Nawab of Bhopal had Partition not intervened. With regard to Qudsiya's reign, Shaharyar Khan writes, 'She introduced administrative reforms that helped effective governance of the state. She led her armies by example; riding out into the field to counter skirmishes ... She built the Moti Masjid (Pearl Mosque) and a number of other buildings in the city. She broke new ground by employing a British engineer to construct a water pipeline that provided drinking water to the people of Bhopal. Later in life, she negotiated a railway through Bhopal and provided funds from her personal account, as distinct from state funds, for the construction of part of the railway. ... Above all, Qudsiya Begum's rule initiated Bhopal into the tradition of simple living, close contact between ruler and subject, Hindu-Muslim harmony and a deliberate avoidance of the opulence, pomp and decadence normally associated with Indian princely states.'

As mentioned earlier, Qudsiya had announced the betrothal of her daughter Sikandar to Munir, the son of her principal rival to the throne Amir Mohammad. As the years went by and the time neared for Sikandar to attain the age of maturity, Amir and his son Munir agitated for an early marriage. This would have meant Qudsiya relinquishing power to the new Nawab. She first declared that Sikandar was too young to marry and then went on postponing the event on one excuse or another. Amir and Munir then hatched a plot to overthrow Qudsiya and took to arms. Qudsiya's devoted supporter Balthazar de Bourbon led the Bhopal forces and there was a four day skirmish. Balthazar won the day, captured Munir and threw him at Qudsiya's feet to beg forgiveness.

The British, alarmed by this encounter, intervened. They now pressed Qudsiya to fix the date of marriage. She was however, loath to do so and played another trump card. She falsely declared that Munir was impotent! She based this charge on the evidence of a courtesan. It was then decided that Munir's younger brother, Jahangir be selected as Sikandar's husband.Since Jahangir was a few years younger than his brother, Qudsiya could again postpone the marriage. Finally however the British had enough of Qudsiya's procrastination and the Governor-General Lord Bentinck ordered an early marriage. Thus without further ado, the marriage was celebrated in April 1836.

This was followed by more political turmoil. Now there were three rivals at the Bhopal court: Qudsiya Begum, her daughter Sikandar and her husband Jahangir. Qudsiya however continued to cling to power. This resulted in a civil war, with

Sikandar siding with her mother. Qudsiya's trusted minister Raja Khushwakt Rai led the Bhopal forces, actively helped by Sikandar. Jahangir was defeated and imprisoned for two months. The British then stepped in and a contingent of their army arrived in Bhopal. Qudsiya was finally cornered and it was then that she decided to hand over power. The British gave her a vast *jagir* to which she retired. Jahangir Mohammad was invested as the Nawab in November 1837.

Qudsiya lived up to the age of eighty, always retaining her devout and austere way of life. Jahangir was a total failure and ruled only for a few years. He was weak and debauched and his wife Sikandar not only left him for a while, but being a strong willed woman she terrorised him 'with gunfire and cavalry charges'. He was, at one stage, actually, captured and imprisoned but the British insisted on his release. Jahangir and his family then attempted to assassinate Sikandar and Jahangir was charged to perform the evil deed. Primed with alcohol, he crept up the staircase to her chamber and swinging wildly with his sword, he only managed to injure her before fleeing.

Jahangir's decadent existence led to serious illness and he was another of the many nawabs who died young, at the age of twenty-seven. This resulted in the usual squabbles for the throne and even a short civil war. Amir Mohammad, Jahangir's father, once again took to arms. He took into service a hundred Rohila Pathans and captured a fort near Bhopal. A British contingent then marched from nearby Sehore to Bhopal and made short work of Amir's force and imprisoned him for life.

*Sikandar Begum*

The British then decided that Sikandar Begum who was 'vigilant, active and a supporter of the English' be appointed as regent, until her eight-year-old daughter Shah Jahan came of age, at which time her future husband would be appointed as the nawab. It was almost a replay of the Qudsiya Begum situation. Thus Sikandar Begum was the regent for twenty-one years from 1847 to 1868.

Shaharyar Khan writes about his ancestor Sikandar Begum, 'Square-jawed, muscular, handsome and with those piercing eyes, Sikandar's personality was over-powering. She rode, played polo, went tiger hunting. ... She rode out to distant villages to take personal stock of her agrarian reform and the welfare of the village folk. She commanded the army and personally inspected the court. ... Sikandar was a devout Muslim but did not take to the veil.'

After her accession to the throne Sikandar Begum initiated a number of reforms. She divided the state into three districts and twenty-one sub districts and appointed *nazims* (revenue officers) to administer each district. She constructed boundary pillars and demarcated the state frontiers for the first time. The begum introduced a judicial system and compiled a code of laws. She set up a separate police force and an intelligence network and also introduced a nominated parliament.

Sikandar paid considerable attention to educational institutions and encouraged scholars to settle in Bhopal. However she tended to follow an Islamic line and renewed the madrasa system (religious school). She admired the Mughals and aimed at some kind of Mughal Renaissance.

Sikandar reorganised the army which had a strength of 4,265 soldiers including a cavalry force of about 500. Importantly, she ended the system of contingents being supplied by vassals and replaced it with regular salaries for her army. This meant an annual expenditure of almost rupees three lakhs. Work on the railway line which would link Bhopal to the national network continued. But both Qudsiya and she had died before the first locomotive steamed into the state capital in 1882.

By 1854, Sikandar's only daughter Shah Jahan was sixteen years old and her mother decided to get her married. Unlike her mother, Shah Jahan was attractive and

entirely feminine. Many Bhopal Pathan families were considered but were ultimately rejected. Sikandar then took permission from the British government to look outside the state, but none of the candidates were suitable, although the pretty Shah Jahan enjoyed brief flirtatious romances with some. Ultimately the begum selected the grizzled middle-aged commander-in-chief of the Bhopal army, Baqi Mohammad Khan and ordered him to marry her young daughter. Baqi begged that the begum not insist as he already had children of Shah Jahans age and to drive home the fact 'he sent a silver tray to Sikandar Begum carrying his bottle of hair dye, false teeth and spectacles'. Unmoved, she insisted that the marriage take place. Sikandar Begum surmised that Baqi would pose no threat to her own rule. He was loyal and would not repeat the folly of sons-in-law of previous generations and demand that he be made nawab. The petite Shah Jahan and Baqi had two daughters, one of who, in due course became the fourth Begum of Bhopal.

When the Revolt of 1857 engulfed the northern and central parts of the sub-continent, it was touch and go whether the British would be able to suppress the uprising. In the nearby towns of Sehore and Berasia, the *sipahis* of the British contingent, took to arms and killed some British officers and captured the cannons. During this critical time Sikandar backed the winning horse. She gave shelter to escaping British officers and their families and sent loyal elements in her army to help out the foreigner. She also sent supplies of grains and other forage as far as Kalpi near Kanpur, where the Rani of Jhansi and Tatya Tope were valiantly fighting the British enemy. For this succour, Sikandar earned the undying gratitude of her masters.

In 1858, young Shah Jahan gave birth to a daughter whom she named Sultan Jahan. Thus four generations of the ruling family of Bhopal had produced only girls. It was also extraordinary, as Shaharyar Khan points out that 'four consecutive women rulers were alive at the same time'—Qudsiya, Sikandar, Shah Jahan and Sultan Jahan.

After the Revolt of 1857, Sikandar Begum saw the opportunity of being appointed regent for life. She was only forty-one and in her prime. She based her claim to the

*Shah Jahan and Sultan Jahan*

British on her loyal services during the rebellion. Her other arguments were of a religious nature, as the Koran did not forbid women's rule. This placed the British in a dilemma, as Shah Jahan had come of age. The problem was solved when Shah Jahan herself waived all rights to the throne during her mother's lifetime. This gesture was viewed generally as one of generosity and kindness. But there were vast differences in the personalities of the mother and daughter. Sikandar was masculine and dominating while Shah Jahan was delicate and feminine. There was thus the theory that Shah Jahan had been forced into abdicating her claim by her mother.

Sikandar was much feted by the British when she attended their durbars held at Jabalpore and Allahabad. While she had dropped purdah at Bhopal, she covered herself at these durbars wearing a burqa with her decorations and jewellery worn on the outside. She also visited Jaipur and Gwalior and was very impressed by the warm and colourful receptions she got from the maharajas, and particularly by the military pageantry on display.

In 1863, Sikandar decided to go on a pilgrimage to Mecca and was the first Muslim ruler to do so. She wrote a book on this experience in which she states that some of her baggage was stolen on arrival and she was not treated politely by the local officials. She wrote that Jeddah was a dirty city with bad drainage. She criticised the Turkish population of Mecca as follows, 'The Turks are very dirty in their habits, and gross livers; … in their houses they are very dirty and untidy in their dress.' She was disappointed by the city of Mecca which she found dirty and unclean while the houses were built on a very unsatisfactory plan. She also used strong words about the Arabs, stating that there was no sincere friendship but only falsehood and intrigue among them. The begum spent almost nine months on her travels.

A couple of years after she returned, she fell seriously ill and died at the comparatively young age of fifty-one.

Meanwhile Shah Jahan's marriage to the middle-aged Baqi was on the point of breaking up. Shah Jahan had several lovers much to the despair of her husband. Thoroughly fed up, Baqi also decided to go on Haj. But soon after his return he died, leaving the begum at the age of twenty-nine, a distinctly merry widow.

A contemporary French traveller Rousselet, who came to Bhopal described Shah Jahan, 'Her face, which was of great beauty, … was lighted by black eyes of a singular expression of pride and determination … One thing alone disfigured her striking countenance, and that was the blackness of the teeth, corroded and roughened by the abuse of betel.'

After Sikandar's death Shah Jahan became the Begum of Bhopal and the British authorities proclaimed that her ten-year-old daughter Sultan Jahan would be the heir apparent. This was premature as Shah Jahan could have remarried and produced a son who would then have had precedence over Sultan Jahan. The British government

*Shah Jahan Begum*

had however given an assurance to Sikandar, the previous begum, that her beloved granddaughter's rights would be protected and what the colonial masters said was law.

In the first years of her reign, Shah Jahan showed much commitment and continued the reforms initiated by her reformist mother. The state treasury was in debit to an amount of rupees five and a half lakhs. This debt was completely paid off in a few years. The people of Bhopal were suffering because of the high price of corn. She abolished the tax on grain and imported it into the city to ameliorate their lot. She also initiated the cultivation of opium in the state and in a few years it became an important source of revenue. It is seldom realised that the British were the biggest drug mafia of all time, forcing it on China.

In 1869, Shah Jahan undertook the long journey to Calcutta to attend the Viceregal Durbar. She was treated with great consideration there and had the time of her life in the metropolis.

The ten-year-old Sultan Jahan moved to her mother's palace and found the atmosphere very different from what she had been used to at her grandmother Sikandar's place. The sobriety was gone and there was much cheer all round. There were *mushairas* where famous poets recited their latest compositions. There was music and dancing and everyone was enjoying the good life. Shah Jahan Begum became a patron of the arts and many poets and scholars were at her court. She was a writer and a poet herself and wrote several books in Urdu as well as composed poems of some merit under the pen name 'Shirin'. She even compiled two dictionaries which contained selected terms not only in Urdu, Arabic and Persian but also Hindi and Sanskrit.

Shah Jahan also had many admirers and lovers, whose company she enjoyed. She however became bewitched by one man Siddiq Hassan. He arrived in Bhopal from Uttar Pradesh and started by selling *ittar* (perfume) and was described as 'poor as a church mouse' and an 'impecunious non-Pathan clerk'. But he was intelligent and knowledgeable. He got a job as a lowly clerk but climbed the administrative ladder quickly and was ultimately appointed as Shah Jahan's private secretary. The relationship between them became too close and finally Shah Jahan became pregnant. This was a

*Siddiq Hassan*

scandalous situation and the British political agent strongly advised the Begum to marry Siddiq Hassan. Shah Jahan was delighted to heed his advice. There was much opposition to the marriage in the Bhopal aristocracy. Qudsiya Begum, who was still alive, thoroughly disapproved not only of the marriage but also Siddiq Hassan. The ruling family was split into two parties.

After the marriage, Siddiq Hasan became the dominant influence in Shah Jahan's life. He persuaded her to give him virtual control of all matters of the state and to negotiate with the British authorities that he be formally given the title of Nawab. This was strongly opposed by the rival faction and the ceremonial procession to mark the event was boycotted by the people of Bhopal.

Siddiq Hassan was a Wahabi Muslim which implied that he was a religious fanatic. Thus according to Wahabi tenets Shah Jahan had to adopt purdah, which she hated but dutifully obeyed. This marriage brought much coldness in Shah Jahan's relations with her daughter Sultan Jahan, the heir apparent, as well as the old grandmother Qudsiya Begum, who was still on the scene. Sultan Jahan always felt that her mother had married much below her own station and someone she described as a 'penniless adventurer'. Sultan Jahan had been betrothed to Ahmad Ali Khan of whom both her mother and Siddiq Hassan disapproved in turn. They humiliated him in various ways which brought further estrangement between mother and daughter. Eventually, Sultan Jahan was married to Ahmad Ali.

During Siddiq Hasan's regime, religious fanaticism was encouraged and there was considerable laxity and corruption in administration. In 1881 there were reports that the Nawab had published seditious material against the British government and was preaching jihad against them. Warning signals were conveyed to Shah Jahan by the British, but she paid scant attention. Finally they took action; a British Resident arrived at Bhopal and held a Durbar at which Shah Jahan and Siddiq Hassan had to be present along with all the Bhopal ministers and noblemen. At this function the Resident praised the reforms introduced by Shah Jahan but he was very critical of Siddiq Hassan. He then announced the deposition of Siddiq Hasan as Nawab and divestment of all honours. He would, in future, have no say in state affairs and all the corrupt officials he had appointed were dismissed. A British administrator was appointed who would run the state, although Shah Jahan remained the ceremonial head. The begum was shattered at this public humiliation, but there was little she could do. Her personal grudge against her daughter Sultan Jahan and her husband increased. She felt that they had both intrigued successfully against her and the British action was the result of their actions. After this incident, Shah Jahan spent several years in attempting to reverse the British goverment's decision against her husband. She made visits to Calcutta to meet the viceroy several times for this purpose, but to no avail. Siddiq Hassan died in 1890, but Shah Jahan continued her effort to have his title of Nawab resumed posthumously and she did succeed a year after his death. That year full executive authority was also restored to Shah Jahan.

The most important development in the remaining years of her life was the connection of Bhopal to the national railway network. This had first been initiated by Qudsiya and followed up by Sikandar. It finally came to fruition now in 1884.

In 1901, after a thirty-three year reign Shah Jahan died of cancer of the mouth, a result of her use of betel for decades. Before she died, however, there was a melancholy reconciliation between her and her daughter Sultan Jahan.

When Sultan Jahan Begum assumed the reins of the government in 1901, she was a matronly forty-three year old. She was rather plain in looks, deeply religious,

*Sultan Jahan Begum*

frugal and craved a simple pious life. In brief, she was quite the opposite of her glamorous and fun-loving mother. Sultan Jahan shunned extravagance and any form of decadence.

On her investiture, Sultan Jahan Begum received gifts from the British government consisting of robes of honour, a pearl necklace, a tiara, a gun and an exquisite sword. Before long they found that Sultan Jahan was a very conscientious and caring ruler. One of the first things she did was to revive the finances of the state, as the treasury was totally empty due to the profligacy of her mother during the last few years of her reign. She even diverted funds from her personal account to the state treasury. Within a few years the state finances were healthy and rising.

Soon after her accession, Sultan Jahan lost her husband Ahmad Ali Khan to heart attack. They had been together for twenty-seven years and it was a great personal tragedy. They had three sons and a daughter.

In 1903, the Begum attended the Coronation Durbar in Delhi and left by special train with 568 retainers. Shaharyar Khan says, 'Not since the heyday of the Moghul Empire, 250 years earlier, had India witnessed such a display of power, pageantry and colonial hauteur. There were early morning duck and partridge shoots, colourful parades and military march-pasts in resplendent uniforms, banquets, garden parties. ... Glamorous rajahs and ranis bedecked in brocade costumes and shimmering jewellery, mingled with British officers dressed in their starched uniforms. Amidst this ceremonial and glittering display of riches, stood the simple, pious Sultan Jahan—dressed in cotton—conversing in broken English ... already the subject of immense respect and admiration at the Viceroy's Court. She was unique not only because she was the only woman ruler at the durbar but because of her serious commitment to the progress of her people and enlightened administration of the state.'

Once Sultan Jahan Begum had established control over state governance and started on her reforms, she decided to go on a pilgrimage to Mecca. She wrote a book on her experience and as the year was 1904, her comments are of interest. After a troublesome sea voyage, she had to travel several hundred miles through the

Arab desert in a litter slung between two camels. Her caravan consisted of 1000 people and hundreds of camels and horses. They were under constant fire from the marauding bedouins and on one occasion she had a narrow escape. She was swindled by camel drivers, stud owners, ship charters and landlords throughout her journey. A bit disillusioned, she returned after many months.

Sultan Jahan's most important reforms related to the upliftment, education and enlightenment of women. She built schools and insisted on high standards. At the beginning of this chapter, I have mentioned my grandfather, who was treated most generously by Sultan Jahan after he had rescued one of the princes from the Bhopal Lake. As part of family memorabilia, I have a copy of the Begum's book *An Account of My Life* printed almost 100 years ago. She has this to say about my grandmother: 'Mrs. Johory (she spells it Mrs. Jowhari) has worked hard and successfully for the institutions under her management. Mrs. Johory has not been long in Bhopal, but has already proved herself a valuable acquisition to the Education Department. I am very grateful to this lady for the work she has done for the cause of female education in Bhopal, a cause which I hold to be my special mission to promote.' The begum's work in women's emancipation and education led to her being appointed as the Chancellor of Aligarh Muslim University, an appointment she held for three terms.

In 1911, the begum went to London to attend the coronation of George V. At the ceremony, she caused mild amusement and received much media attention by appearing in a burqa with her awards worn on the outside. The ill informed press wrote about her having appeared in a dressing gown and went on to add for good measure that she ate a live chicken for dinner!

Over the decades Bhopal had developed a distinctive culture. Urdu was spoken but with a distinctive Bhopali accent, which is recognisable to this day. The men wore *safas* (turbans) tied in the Rajputana style; the favoured colour was turquoise. Aligarhi pajamas, which are popular in North India today, were worn with pump shoes. The Bhopali women had a distinctive and elegant dress. It consisted of a kurta that flared in circles flowing down from a tight-fitting waist. The dupatta was much longer than is usual today and carried across the body and over the shoulder. The women wore *churidars* (tight calf-hugging pajamas) in rich colours.

Of the three sons Sultan Jahan had, her favourite by far was Hamidullah Khan, the youngest. She had taken special pains with his education which was rounded off at Aligarh University. He was a good sportsman and excelled at polo. Even when Hamidullah was a child, Sultan Jahan scouted for a suitable wife for him. She sent an emissary to the Afghanistan frontier and he was enchanted by five-year-old Maimoona Sultan, a descendant of Afghan kings. The child bride Maimoona was brought to Bhopal by Sultan Jahan to be brought up as a model woman. To quote Shaharyar Khan on his grandmother: 'Maimoona Sultan was brought up in the traditional Muslim manner ... but she learnt to ride and shoot ... the critical difference in Maimoona's upbringing was that she was educated to hold her own in a sophisticated Western milieu ... she was thoroughly groomed in Western etiquette, but she could carry herself gracefully in a sari and Muslim dresses. ... By the time she reached adolescence Maimoona Sultan was beautiful, graceful and highly sophisticated—a truly crafted jewel.' Hamid and Maimoona were married around 1912 and had three daughters in the next four years.

*Hamidullah Khan*

In 1924, Sultan Jahan's two elder sons died in quick succession. They were both survived by two sons each. Based on primogeniture, Sultan Jahan's surviving grandsons had a superior claim to the throne, than her own younger son. But she was determined that her favourite son Hamid should succeed her. She scoured the law books and a case was put before the viceroy. After much argument and study, lasting almost a year, the viceroy rejected her case and ruled that her eldest grandson was the rightful heir. Not to be deterred, Sultan Jahan decided to go to London and personally plead her case and fight a lost battle with the British government and King George V. She met the secretary of state and half the cabinet. In her meeting with King George V she made a heart rending appeal, burst into tears and fainted! There was consternation, sympathy and smelling salts to help her recover.

Finally, Hamidullah was officially proclaimed heir apparent in 1926. Sultan Jahan Begum then abdicated in his favour. On the coronation of the new Nawab, a century of women's rule ended. Sultan Jahan died in 1930 after having ruled for twenty-five years. She had brought integrity, fair governance and education to the people of Bhopal, especially the women.

# 7

# Chhattrasal of Bundelkhand

One of the princes of Mahoba, Bundelkhand—the small principality of Chhattrasal—was in school with me. Murli Manohar, the prince in question, once almost saved my life. That weekend the younger boys were doing social work by helping build a road. Totally inexperienced, some boys were swinging their picks rather wildly, while others were collecting the clods in a tray and disposing them. It was my turn to collect the loosened soil but I loafed off and Murli Manohar volunteered to take my turn. The next thing I saw was the point of a pick, clumsily swung by another boy, burying itself in Murli Manohar's skull. There was a sprout of blood and he lay still on the ground. He recovered after several operations but always carried a silver plate in his skull. He often told me that he had saved my life.

Some of the following account is based on the stories this friend told me about his ancestor, but most of it relies on facts as stated by eminent historians. I have also made use of the epic *Chattraprakash* composed by Lal Kavi, a bard at the court of Chhattrasal. Lal Kavi, like a worthy and virtuous court poet, grossly exaggerated Chhattrasal's feats but then what are bards for? They tug at your soul and bring tears to your eyes which historians seldom can! One has, however, to sift through and often discount the poet's hyperbole. Nevertheless, *Chattraprakash* is still noteworthy, not only as a source of historical facts, but also as poetry in the heroic tradition.

In 1882, almost a century after Chhattrasal, Pogson wrote *A History of the Boondelas*, and although he quotes from *Chattraprakash* he also states that, 'Some parts of the work are extremely obscure and unintelligible.'

Bundelkhand is a tract of land which slopes from the Vindhya mountains in Central India to the river Yamuna in the north. It is bounded on the west by the road from Agra to Gwalior and on the east by the Kaimur Range. In this area were situated the old princely states of Jhansi, Orchha, Datia, Panna, Banda, Rewa and other minor ones. The country is wild and rugged and was at that time thickly forested. Many a hilltop were crowned by formidable and picturesque fortresses built by the Bundela and Maratha chieftains. As these strongholds were difficult to subdue, after the Revolt of 1857, the British demolished several of them. This was vandalism of the highest degree because some of these ancient fortresses were of great historical and architectural interest.

The area took its name from its dominant race—the Bundelas—a clan of Gaharwar Rajputs, who, like some other Rajput clans, trace their mythical genealogy to Ram. War was their main occupation, their sole means of earning glory and riches and their only amusement. They carried on running battles with the Mughals over several decades and were only subdued during the reign of Jahangir and Shah Jahan. The local chieftains finally succumbed and accepted the lordship of the Mughals in return of being permitted to enjoy being the rajas of their little principalities. However, the noblest of

*Chhatris of the Bundela rulers across the Betwa River, Orchha*

the Bundela Rajputs, Champat Rai and his son Chhattrasal, refused to bow down to the imperial government. Their small principality of Mahoba, sheltered within a network of ravines, rose to prominence in the latter half of the seventeenth century when Champat Rai and Chhattrasal continued the wars for over five decades. They devastated territory loyal to the Mughals and spread havoc and chaos over the land till in the next century, a mightier race of plunderers appeared on the scene—the Marathas. Peshwa Baji Rao marched to Bundelkhand and helped Chhattrasal (who was then an old man but still fighting) in repelling a final attack by the Mughals in 1727.

Champat Rai Bundela was a petty chieftain, but he raised the standard of rebellion against the mighty Emperor Shah Jahan and raided several Mughal outposts. The local Mughal *faujdar* (commander) along with the Raja of Orchha, acted against Champat Rai, but their joint campaign was soon in disarray because of the stubborn resistance put up by the gallant rebel. After some years of these hit and run tactics, Champat Rai thought it prudent to make overtures to the Mughal court, whereupon he was summoned to Delhi and enlisted in imperial service. In 1856, he was one of the commanders in the siege of Kandahar, in Afghanistan. For his meritorious service he was awarded a *jagir* in the district of Kunch, which was near his principality and worth a tidy sum of rupees three lakhs a year. However, sometime later due to the intrigues of the Raja of Orchha, Champat was deprived of his *jagir*. He left Delhi in disgust, reverted to his rebellious ways and continued his guerilla warfare for several years. He and his family were constantly on the move and always in peril. Finally, Champat was felled by treachery and his wife, Kali Kunwar who came to his aid, was also killed.

Chhattrasal thus lost both his parents on the same day. He was only eleven years old and was overwhelmed with grief. However, he had three older brothers to nurture him but the next few years, of which we know little, must have been difficult. We next hear of Chhattrasal as a young man described as being 'powerful as a tiger and an expert in the use of the matchlock, the sword and the spear'. He was also a splendid horseman and as he sped past, swift as the wind, people wondered at his skill. He was excellent at *choghan* (polo) and was also a keen hunter, taking special delight in hunting deer with cheetahs. His talents were not limited to the purely physical, for intellectually too he was exceptional and was deeply interested in literature and poetry as was evinced by his association with Lal Kavi.

For several years before his death, Chhattrasal's father, Champat Rai, had raided many neighbouring Bundela chiefs for their loyalty to the Mughals as freely as he had attacked the Mughals themselves. His sons, therefore, had few friends and found no honourable career open to them anywhere in Bundelkhand. They ran out of money and had to sell their mother's jewels. Chhattrasal and his elder brother, Angad Rai, then decided to seek help elsewhere. Before they set out, however, Lal Kavi says that Chhattrasal was 'married to a beautiful young girl of illustrious descent'. The court poet must obviously have been very impressed, for strangely enough, he eulogised even Chhattrasal's mother-in-law! Chhattrasal's wife accompanied him on his travels and lived in military camps during his various campaigns.

For furthering their careers, Chhattrasal and his brother Angad decided to appeal to Mirza Raja Jai Singh of Amber, who should not be confused with Raja Sawai Jai Singh, also of Amber but who came later in history. The events now being spoken about took place in 1665. Jai Singh I was a distinguished statesman and trusted general of Emperor Aurangzeb. He was a veteran of a hundred battles and had fought for two generations of Mughal emperors in the Deccan, in Afghanistan and even in far away Balk and Badakshan in Central Asia. The last, during Shah Jahan's insane invasion of these parts which ended in disaster. Now at the age of fifty-five, he was still commanding the Mughal forces in the Deccan against the Marathas.

The brothers travelled hundreds of miles making long and difficult marches from Bundelkhand to Jai Singh's camp in the Deccan. Although Mirza Raja received them with courtesy, he was a canny and cautious man and he knew of Aurangzeb's antipathy for Champat Rai because of his marauding ways. But Champat was now dead and in his heart of hearts, Jai Singh had admiration for the way the old man had continued to wage his lone battle against great odds. The two young men who stood before him had nothing to offer except their valour, their talent and their enterprise. Mirza Raja knew their background and pedigree and was sure that they would make valiant warriors. He told them, 'I have heard of your illustrious father and his intrepid fight for a free Bundelkhand. However, you well know that this was against the interests of the Empire and the Emperor will have to be placated. I will, therefore, first employ you in my own contingent and will give you both an appropriate command. If you prove worthy and render good service, I will have a good case for recommending you for enlistment to the imperial army.'

Chhattrasal and Angad, bred as they were to arms, delighted in the scenes of the camp, the tough physical drill, the practice with sword and matchlock and the sound of the warlike *nakkara* (kettledrums). The camps of the time were veritable cities with elaborate tents to house the families and women of the nobles and other tents for thousands of soldiers, merchants and suppliers. The camps extended for miles over the countryside.

Chhattrasal and Angad accompanied Mirza Raja Jai Singh at the siege of Purandar which was held by the Marathas. Both the brothers distinguished themselves in the action, particularly Chhattrasal, who in battle, led the van and was seen in the fiercest of the fighting. Jai Singh kept his word to the two young men and soon he got them *mansabs* (command) of *hazari* (one thousand soldiers) and *teen sadi* (three hundred). The next year they followed Jai Singh in his invasion of Bijapur.

Chhattrasal was next sent by Jai Singh as a part of the detachment which was dispatched to reinforce the Mughal general Diler Khan in his attack on the recalcitrant Raja of Deogarh. The raja had occupied the passes in the hills surrounding Deogarh. The heavy fire from the Mughal artillery compelled him to fall back on the fort of Deogarh. In the ensuing battle, Chhattrasal again distinguished himself. According to Lal Kavi as rendered by Pogson, 'Raja Chhattrasal, valiant in war, dreadful in battle, active, vigorous, penetrated into the midst of the battle, while thousands of balls and arrows discharged at him fell like rain around. He inflicted and received wounds, scattering death and destruction. Kali was delighted to see his sword dance … and the enemy fled like deer from a tiger'. While Chhattrasal fought heroically, Lal Kavi's hyperbole that the Mughal victory was solely due to a charge made by Chhattrasal single handed, must be rejected.

By the evening, the kettledrums and trumpets sounded the strains of victory for the Mughal army. But as night fell and the chiefs assembled to discuss the action of the day, Chhattrasal alone was missing. No one had seen him, and his followers searched in every direction but no trace of him could be found. They spent their whole night in fretless quest; loudly calling 'Chhattrasal' but the echo of the hills was the lone response. They feared the worst and to them victory was like defeat, for Chhattrasal was gone. They did not, however, give up and as dawn was breaking, they saw a horse fully saddled and bridled standing by a young man lying wounded on the ground. They recognised Chhattrasal's charger and on raising the young man, they found that life still remained. He was taken back to the camp, carefully treated and ministered to till he fully recovered.

There were many eyewitness accounts of the bravery Chhattrasal showed on the field of battle. The contribution he made towards the eventual Mughal victory was acknowledged and extolled by all except by the commander, Diler Khan. The latter did not bestow one word of appreciation on Chhattrasal although he even expressed admiration for the instinct of Chhattrasal's horse which had stood alongside his fallen master. When news of the victory reached Aurangzeb, he acclaimed Diler Khan's achievement and increased his *mansab*. Many of the warriors far less worthy than Chhattrasal were also rewarded but there was no praises or advancement for Chhattrasal.

Chhattrasal was disgusted at this treatment and according to the always colourful Lal Kavi, he said, 'Diler Khan was an illiterate yokel, who could not discern the difference between a *kitab* and a *kabab* and displaying one's bravery to an ignoramus like him was like playing a *been* (musical instrument) to a buffalo, or perfuming the body of an ass, or showing pictures to the blind.' He therefore decided to quit the service of such a fool.

In any case service in the imperial army did not offer scope for Chhattrasal's soaring ambition. He dreamt of independence from the Mughal yoke and his thoughts turned to the great Maratha leader Shivaji, who had successfully defied Aurangzeb and made the Mughal generals bite the dust. Shivaji had by now captured much territory in Maharashtra and controlled many fortresses.

Chhattrasal decided to seek out Shivaji, and accompanied by his young wife and his loyal followers, he left the Mughal camp for the ostensible purpose of hunting deer. The journey was several hundred miles long and perilous, through unfamiliar territory, but Chhattrasal and his party traversed the fortress and hills of the Deccan. Finally they reached Shivaji's domain and established camp near Sinhgarh, one of Shivaji's strongholds.

On getting an appointment to meet Shivaji, young Chhattrasal rode slowly up the steep and tortuous path leading to Sinhgarh Fort where Shivaji had encamped. Bundelkhand had many splendid forts, with Kalinjar being the most noteworthy, but Chhattrasal, seeing the design and construction of Sinhgarh, surmised that this was one of the most powerful forts he had seen. Surrounded by sheer cliffs, the strong fort

*Jai Singh meeting Shivaji before the Treaty of Purandar*

walls with bastions at intervals, wound along the hillsides. Thus the fort was defended not only by nature but also by fortifications. Chhattrasal followed the path uphill, passing six huge defending gates ranged in succession rising to the fort on the summit. Each of the gates had massive doors plated and studded with iron spikes. He was greeted by guards in Maratha uniforms, the blades of their swords glistening in the sunlight and finally found himself in the presence of the great Shivaji. The latter rose at Chhattrasal's approach and received him with honour and distinction. He seated Chhattrasal next to himself and courteously enquired about the reason for the arduous journey. Chhattrasal poured out his heart and related the events which had led him to quit Bundelkhand. Shivaji listened attentively to Chhattrasal's

*Entrance to Sinhgarh fort*

account of his battles and achievements and his burning desire to serve Shivaji. Chhattrasal said, 'Maharaja, I have traversed the country and come to you because you are the one hope of achieving our independence. You have set such a noble example of heroism and fortitude. There is nothing in the world I would desire more than to offer my services and fight alongside you.'

Shivaji remained in thought for some time. He liked and admired the young man's spirit and enterprise and finally said, 'My brave friend, conquer and subdue your foes! Destroy the imperial army; slay the Turks and the Mughals. There are many of those races that have struck at me but on them I have tried the temper of my blade and slain them. But you must return immediately to your native Bundelkhand; use your local influence and raise an army, grasp the sword and god will assist you in your endeavours. This way we will help each other far more than by your remaining by my side. The Turk cannot fight in several places at the same time. We will each distract the enemy when he is active in your country or in mine. Thus we will subvert their plans by active cooperation.'

As Chhattrasal pondered on these words, Shivaji further counselled him, 'You must understand that if you are victorious in your own country and regain your independence, your name will be enshrined in history. If, however, you fight by my side and we destroy the enemy in Maharashtra, the glory will be mine. So go back to your dominion and god will guide you to victory and independence.' Shivaji then took off his sword and girded it on Chhattrasal. As Chhattrasal departed, inspired by Shivaji, great dreams and lofty ambitions filled his mind.

Before returning to Bundelkhand, he first visited Subhakaran, the Raja of Datia, who like Chhattrasal, was a Bundela. In Mughal employ and posted in the Deccan at the head of a large contingent of his clansmen, Subhakaran was a loyal officer of the Mughals and regarded with favour by Emperor Aurangzeb. Subhakaran expressed pleasure at meeting Chhattrasal and was very hospitable. Chhattrasal stayed at his camp for some time but despite all his eloquence he could not sway Subhakaran. The latter was astonished at Chhattrasal's bold ideas but felt that Chhattrasal's plan of a rising in Bundelkhand against the Mughals was not only reckless but also an absurd dream. His own loyalty could not be shaken and he was happy to be in Mughal service. However, Subhakaran offered to plead Chhattrasal's case with the emperor and obtain a suitable rank for him. Chhattrasal replied spiritedly, 'I had earlier accepted a *mansab* and served the Mughals, but I don't think I can ever rely on them. I have at present no army and little following, but I will get back home and you will see what I can do. Even if the armies of the emperor are as overwhelming as the waves of the ocean. I am determined to face and defeat them and happen what may, I will remain independent.'

Accompanied by his wife and his small band of followers, Chhattrasal once again crossed the Narmada and returned to Bundelkhand. The year was 1670 and Chhattrasal was twenty-one years old. Now commenced a struggle that was to last over half a century. Chhattrasal had with him five horsemen and twenty-five foot soldiers. It seemed to all that Chhattrasal without troops, without treasure, without a stronghold or even country could not attack the mighty Mughal Empire, one of the richest and strongest empires in the world at the time, with the slightest hope of success.

About this time, however, one of those quirks of fate came to the aid of Chhattrasal. This was Aurangzeb's blind fanaticism which played right into the hands of the passionate young Bundela patriot. Aurangzeb embarked on a policy of crushing the Hindus, destroying their temples or converting them into mosques and mutilating their beautifully sculpted idols. As the tyrant said, 'When their temples no longer exist, their faith will dwindle away.' This created an ideal opening for Chhattrasal because the Hindus were shaken to the core by this sacrilege. The population of Bundelkhand and the neighbouring province of Malwa took to arms in defence of their honour and the altar of their gods. They longed for a bold leader who would repeat Champat Rai's spirited defiance of the Mughals and protect their religion. Fidai Khan was then the governor of Gwalior and he received orders from Delhi to demolish the temple at Orchha in the heartland of Bundelkhand. Fidai Khan, apprehending trouble from the warlike Bundela Rajputs, collected a strong imperial force and unfurled his standard at Dhoomghat. The valiant Raja Dharmangad at the head of a Bundela army attacked Fidai Khan and 'like an enraged tiger amid a herd of elephants, slew many and obtained a signal victory'.

The feelings of all were so outraged by Aurangzeb's hare-brained attack on their religion that even those who had for so long loyally served the ungrateful Mughal government, now transferred their sympathies to their rebel brethren and resolved to act along with them. Chhattrasal decided to take full advantage of this situation, but the canny man that he was, he knew that effective action against the Mughals would require long and careful preparations. He was after all taking on the greatest monarch of that age. He once again decided to approach Subhakaran who had earlier rejected Chhattrasal's proposal to rebel, and who had since returned home to Bundelkhand after campaigning in the Deccan on behalf of Aurangzeb. Full of resentment at the emperor's anti-Hindu policy and encouraged by the defeat of Fidai Khan's imperial army at Dhoomghat, this time Subhakaran threw in his lot with Chhattrasal. Subhakaran knew of Chhattrasal's father brave efforts and had faith in Chhattrasal's destiny of leading them to independence.

As the next step in his preparation to face the might of the empire, Chhattrasal travelled to Aurangabad and visited Beer Baldev. Like the people of Bundelkhand, Baldev was also hoping that a leader would arise to defy Aurangzeb's fanatic decree and protect the Hindu religion. Baldev agreed to be Chhattrasal's partner in the projected war against the Mughals. He assured Chhattrasal that he and his men would hold themselves

in readiness and would join the movement. As Baldev eloquently put it, 'You Chhattrasal are predestined like the moon to illumine the world. Your follower like the stars to accompany your career of glory.'

Having made certain of this ally, Chhattrasal once again crossed the Narmada and re-entered Bundelkhand. He visited his brother, Ratan Shah, who held some territory at Bichhuri near Chhattarpur, and asked him to join in the war. Chhattrasal said to him, 'My brother we will have the whole of Bundelkhand behind us and if we have initial success and overwhelm the enemy and lay waste imperial territory, not just Bundelkhand but the whole country will rise in arms in defence of the faith.'

Ratan Shah was not convinced and replied, 'Think some more my brother, think of the might of the emperor's army, think of his enormous wealth and resources. Compare that with your feeble means of opposition. This is a mad man's dream. Who will protect you?'

Chhattrasal replied, 'My protector is the Almighty.' For eighteen days Chhattrasal entreated his brother to join him, but for Ratan Shah, fighting Aurangzeb was a hopeless task. Chhattrasal had to return without his brother by his side.

Chhattrasal, however, had help in men and arms both from Subhakaran and Beer Baldev. The latter joined by Baqi Khan, who is called a Bundela in the Hindi poem, but who, Sir J.N. Sarkar, the eminent historian, surmises was 'an Afghan brigand chief settled in the district and a natural enemy of the Mughal and indeed of every orderly government.' The rebels elected Chhattrasal as their leader and king of all the Bundelas, with a right to 55 per cent of the booty, while Baldev was to get the remaining 45 per cent. Chhattrasal's army was still a tiny force counted in hundreds, but he soon received large reinforcements. The soldiers who had fought for Champat Rai, and who had so long remained without work, now hastened from all over Bundelkhand to the standard of his son at the thought of plunder and fortune. In addition, Hindus, in general, who felt strongly about Aurangzeb's policy of destroying temples, flocked to join Chhattrasal, hailing him as the champion of the Hindu faith and Kshatriya honour.

The war which was to last half a century thus began. As Chhattrasal advanced into Bundelkhand at the head of this rebel force, the chiefs living on the path of his advance and who were cordial to his cause, agreed to join him. Other chiefs who did not, had to face Chhattrasal in battle and were easily routed and their lands plundered. Among the latter was the Raja of Dhureer, who influenced by animosity against Chhattrasal's father, drew out his troops to oppose the advance. Chhattrasal demolished the raja's forces, plundered the town of Dhureer and compelled the raja to sue for terms.

As Chhattrasal continued his advance, he was opposed by the combined forces of Hashim Khan, a Mughal *faujdar* and Anand Rai, a local raja. Receiving advance intelligence of this and knowing that the Afghans were brave adversaries, Chhattrasal did not hazard a general action. Instead he placed a part of his troops in ambush and by gradual retreat drew the enemy into the ambuscade. The surprise was total and numerous Afghans fell. Panic prevailed among the rest and they fled without stopping until they reached Sironj.

Several other engagements took place, the most noteworthy one being against Sayyid Bahadur, another Mughal *faujdar*, who with his Mughal and Afghan troops, attacked Chhattrasal. In the ensuing battle many gallant charges were made but the Mughals were driven off the field and pursued by the Bundelas as far as the town of Sindh, which they first plundered and then razed its fortifications to the ground. Chhattrasal advanced further and ransacked the important town of Gwalior.

As Lal Kavi says, 'With a thousand tongues did rumour then, the fame of Champat's son through distant lands repeat.' Thus Chhattrasal's fame had spread to distant parts of the country and his repeated successes motivated those who had been wavering earlier, to join him. Many rajas, including his brother Ratan Shah and even Durjan Sal, the ruler of Bundi in Rajputana, allied themselves with the rebels of Bundelkhand and now Chhattrasal found himself at the head of a powerful army commanded by seventy zealous and valiant chiefs. Artillery, cavalry and infantry assembled round the standard of Chhattrasal. He also started to follow the Maratha system of sparing the places that paid him one-fourth of their *chauth* (revenue) and plundering those that refused or resisted.

At this stage of his career, Chhattrasal's raids were directed mostly against the Dhamoni region as well as the rich city of Sironj, which lay 105 kilometres west of it. Successive Mughal *faujdars* of Dhamoni resisted him but were usually defeated and only on rare occasions could they boast of victory.

One of these *faujdars*, Khaliq, was captured by Chhattrasal and held to a ransom of Rs. 30,000. But the people of the district refused to pay up. Chhattrasal then demanded and obtained an order on Keshav Rai Bundela, an official in the Mughal service, who collected the revenue of Bansa area. When this was presented to this chief, Keshav Rai hurled it on the ground, ran it through with his sword and, shouting defiance, prepared for war.

Chhattrasal's encounter with Keshav Rai, which followed, was quite extraordinary as it was decided by single combat. On hearing of Keshav Rai's reaction, Chhattrasal marched towards Bansa. Keshav Rai Bundela drew up his troops in front of Chhattrasal's and arrogantly boasted, 'Where is Chhattrasal? Let him advance and I will put his skill and courage to the test. He calls himself a Kshatriya, let him show his prowess.'

*Kalinjar fort, 1814*

Chhattrasal heard this proud challenge and galloping in front of Keshav Rai, exclaimed, 'Proud chief, advance. You will have the advantage of the first assault. You are now at liberty to take it with sword, matchlock, spear or arrow.'

During this spirited exchange the confronting troops stood in mute and breathless expectation. To quote Lal Kavi, 'On the arm at length, did Keshav Rai strike Chhattrasal, who his skill applauded; then his lance discharging full on the side, that chief he struck. Recovering from the blow, Keshav Rai, his brilliant bladed saber drew and fiercely rushed on Chhattrasal, who cool, collected, sure, a proper time awaiting, continued but to parry, until at length, a blow he struck across the face of Keshav Rai, penetrating deep within the skull. Prompt from his horse that chief was hurled and to the shades departed.'

Twenty years passed in this never-ceasing struggle. In the course of his career Chhattrasal defeated many Mughal commanders, several of whom are listed in Irvine's *Later Mughals*. However, it would serve no purpose to go into the details of every battle. Aurangzeb sent several expeditions against the Bundela king but to no avail. One of these Mughal expeditions interrupted Chhattrasal's marriage ceremony(most probably his second marriage). Arrayed in nuptial garments Chhattrasal was walking with his bride seven times round the fire when the Mughals commenced their attack. Undaunted, Chhattrasal persevered in completing his marriage rites and then joined the battle. Some descriptions of this battle are worth quoting. 'Bullets and arrows fell like rain. The volleys from the matchlock were like a tiger's roar. With thundering peal the cannons echoed; and from the clouds of smoke, the orbs of day concealing, rockets like forked lightning sprang ... Like locusts, arrows flew. Dead bodies strewed the hill whence rushed down streams of blood.' Lal Kavi's poetic and melodramatic descriptions of this action ended in victory for his king. In this battle Chhattrasal's allies Beer Baldev and Subhakaran of Datia distinguished themselves while 'Raja Bahoo furiously charged the enemy and on his person brought away many a deep cut, honour's scars.' But many Bundela chiefs 'clad in death garments obtained their heavenly destiny through the solar orb' (A curious and interesting local concept is that the brave enter heaven through the fiery gate of the sun, while the pious enter through the cool moon).

Years passed and Chhattrasal still remained unsubdued. Aurangzeb became increasingly involved in the endless wars in the Deccan against Shivaji and his local commanders in central and northern India grew weaker and more helpless. Chhattrasal obtained many brilliant triumphs including the capture of the great fort of Kalinjar and the area of Dhamoni. He gradually extended his raids and the whole area from the Yamuna in the north to the Rajput border on the west and the Narmada in the south was his happy hunting ground. The capture of Kalinjar was particularly noteworthy as it was an extremely powerful fort. Chhattrasal had to besiege it for eighteen days and lost a large number of troops before this

Laldarwaza, *the sixth gate of Kalinjar fort*

stronghold could be captured. At one point in the siege, the Bundelas had to collect the bodies of the slain and form them into a breastwork of defence against the enemy's heavy fire. The smell from the rotting bodies of their companions was vile, but they provided protection.

The emperor, busy in the Deccan, received intelligence of the several defeats suffered by his commanders at the hands of Chhattrasal and was very disturbed. Here I bring in Lal Kavi's colourful prose again.

> In order to restore the fame and glory of his arms, he ordered his Turkish army to take the field. The proud Turks played their martial bands proceeding to the seat of war and, at a place named Bussea, were met by Chhattrasal. On one side were men; on the other, Bundelas. The flame of war was kindled, and with impetuous fury blazed! The thunder of the cannon, the roaring of the matchlocks, and the rushing noise of rockets; the confusion, clamour, havoc, and destruction which prevailed rendered the field dreadful as the Day of Judgment! The noble chiefs and mighty warriors of Chhattrasal, with the utmost vigour and impetuosity assailed the foe. Slaughter spread: Bundelas fell! The Moosulmans who, displaying valour, came in front, promptly were attacked by Chhattrasal and compelled to recede. A vast explosion then ensued! A spark had fallen in the enemy's magazine! The smoke in murky columns rose, concealed the sun, and darkness enveloped the ensanguined. Prompt through the smoky cloud, the impetuous charge of brave Bundelas rushed: confusion and dismay prevailed among the Turks and precipitate they fled ... Abandoned by the Turks was the long contested field, and in promiscuous flight, their proud host destroyed. The glory, fame, and renown of mighty Chhattrasal, now spread throughout the land; fear, dismay, and dread pervading the imperial chiefs. When the Emperor

> received intelligence of this disaster, his heart within him shrunk; consternation filled his mind.

After the death of Aurangzeb, Bahadur Shah ascended the throne. The new emperor decided to come to terms with Chhattrasal and by 1708, the two had established cordial relations, with Chhattrasal's sons receiving *mansabs* from the emperor. In 1710, Chhattrasal took part alongside the Mughals in the assault on the Lohgarh in the outer Himalayas, where they marched to suppress the Sikh leader Banda Bahadur.

Chhattrasal was now getting on in years and he and his family, probably for the first time in their lives, enjoyed a period of peace. But this was not to last long. After the fall of the Sayyid brothers at Delhi, Emperor Mohammad Shah sent Mohammad Khan Bangash, an Afghan and one of the few seasoned generals of the empire and loyal to the imperial cause, as governor of Allahabad in 1720. Within the limits of Allahabad province lay the greater part of Bundelkhand territory which was held by Chhattrasal, a fact greatly resented by Mohammad Shah. Chhattrasal also made himself thoroughly obnoxious to the imperialists by aiding rebels in the Ganges-Yamuna *doab* region. Mohammad Khan Bangash was, therefore, ordered to mount a major expedition against Chhattrasal. Bangash first sent a force under Diler Khan in May 1721 but this was beaten back by Chhattrasal with Diler Khan and hundreds of his men slain. Bangash then personally led an army across the Yamuna but the Bundelas resisted ferociously and Mohammad Khan had to withdraw after six months of fighting. Chhattrasal, by now an old man but still vigorous of limb and always ready for a good fight, decided to carry the fight into the enemy territory. He overran Bagelkhand right up to the borders of the province of Patna.

Six years later, in 1727, Mohammad Khan was once again ordered to proceed against Chhattrasal. He collected a large force composed mainly of Afghans, his clansmen, and obtained a train of artillery by stripping his fortresses. With this well equipped army they succeeded in clearing the eastern part of Bundelkhand and advanced towards the heartland of Chhattrasal's kingdom. Here both sides suffered heavy losses and many were killed and wounded. Chhattrasal, his sons and his grandsons were forced back to the forests near Jaitpur, where the rugged country and the thick forest cover made any action against them difficult. However, after a month's fighting, the imperial army broke through the Bundela defences and occupied Mahoba and several other forts. The monsoons then put a stop to further military action. However, fighting resumed in winter and after four months Jaitpur fell to the Mughals. Even at the age of eighty, Chhattrasal took part in every battle and fought for every inch of land. This campaign had lasted a full twenty-four months from January 1727 to December 1728.

To give some idea of the intensity of fighting. I quote an excerpt from a report by Mohammad Khan Bangash to the Mughal Emperor.

> Then three strong (Bundela) divisions united together and bore down on our right wing. Many of our men failed to withstand this onset; they began to give way.... In a short time victory would have been with the enemy. Then ... I remembered my reputation as a soldier and my devotion to His Majesty's service ... there was nothing left except to advance in person and fight like a soldier. ... I collected the artillery ... and followed by a few of my best cavalry, I drove my elephant straight into the thick of the enemy, where my men seemed to be struggling hopelessly. The whole of my friends and chelas then performed prodigies of valour in the vangvard, and many received repeated wounds. With the greatest effort the force in front of us had been repulsed.... By God's help and His Majesty's good fortune, after much fighting and slaughter, such as cannot be detailed in this brief report, the whole of the enemy finally withdrew.

Mohammad Khan also mentioned in his report that the Bundela forces were led by Chhattrasal's son, while the eighty-year-old Chhattrasal himself fought in person along with his sons and grandsons. Three generations were fighting in the same battle.

Chhattrasal was in dire straits and finally he surrendered Jaitpur to the enemy along with himself and his family. They were confined to the Mughal camp. Mohammad Khan Bangash established himself at Jaitpur, but little did he realise that his troubles were just beginning. Peshwa Baji Rao, the great Maratha general was not far from Bundelkhand when he heard of Chhattrasal's sad plight. Chhattrasal had sent his emissaries to Baji Rao to come to his assistance without a moment's delay. Chhattrasal's appeal was said to have been couched in these words, 'Know you Baji Rao that I am in the same sad plight in which the famous elephant Gajendra was when caught by the crocodile. My valiant race is on the point of extinction. Come and save my honour.' Baji Rao at once decided to go to the succour of Chhattrasal. Hawk eyed as always, Baji Rao perhaps also saw, at the same time, a fine opportunity to advance his long term design of assailing northern India.

Bangash had kept a strong guard on Chhattrasal, his sons and grandsons. But one night, they got hold of weapons, overpowered the guards and stormed their way out of the Mughal camp. They headed straight for Baji Rao, who was advancing rapidly with a strong cavalry force towards Jaitpur. The Bundela Rajputs joined the advancing Marathas and guided Baji Rao through the forests and mountains of that wild country. Mohammad Khan, meanwhile, was resting from his labours during the recent battles and the Marathas were within two and twenty miles of his camp before he woke up to their approach.

In the ensuing battle, Baji Rao inflicted a complete defeat on Bangash and the latter retreated with the survivors to the fort of Jaitpur. The Maratha and Bundela allies then besieged him and reduced him to the greatest distress. There were no stores or food in the fort and for two months the Afghans had to subsist on the flesh of camels and horses. Men died of starvation; many deserted; all who gave up their arms were allowed to leave. Irvine in his *Later Mughals* states, 'In this time of dire distress Mohammad Khan called up on the Emperor and the great nobles to extricate him. Not a hand was raised to help or encourage him. The Emperor did indeed order the first Bakhshi, Khan Dauran Samsam-ud-daulah, to proceed to Jaitpur. As usual, with this noble, there was much promise and little performance. His advance tents were sent outside the walls of Delhi with great pomp and ceremony; but not one single other step did he take to forward the matter ... he every evening put off his start to the morning, and every morning put it off until the evening.' Khan Dauran did not stir out of Delhi but instead wrote to Chhattrasal that as Mohammad Khan was in his control, he should slay him.

Bangash was saved from this intolerable situation by the efforts of his wife and his son Qaim Khan. They first threw themselves in vain at the foot of the throne and asked for reinforcements. The wife then sent her veil around among the Rohilla nobles and Qaim Khan appealed to them with the eloquence of despair. Qaim then managed to raise a force of 30,000 men and crossed the Yamuna, hastening to the deliverance of his father. But the Marathas intervened and successfully prevented Qaim Khan from affecting a junction with his father and routed him near Jaitpur. Pilaji Jadav, who was accompanying Baji Rao, wrote in a letter, 'Qaim Khan with 30,000 men came against us. We fought him at Supa. By God's grace he was defeated. We captured 3,000 horses and 13 elephants...'

Meanwhile, the monsoons were approaching and it was time for the annual return of the Marathas to their homes. Chhattrasal, therefore, decided it was prudent to come to terms and Mohammad Khan was allowed to evacuate Jaitpur on signing a written agreement that he would never again return to Bundelkhand or give any trouble to Chhattrasal.

The old Bundela king re-entered his capital in full state, amidst the welcoming cheers of the citizens and the boom of the victorious Maratha cannons. Baji Rao left Jaitpur for Pune in May 1729 and with him went Mastani, Chhattrasal's young and beautiful daughter.

Chhattrasal was so grateful to Baji Rao for the help rendered to him and his family that he left a third of his dominions to Baji Rao. These lay in the western part of Bundelkhand and included Jhansi, Sagar, and Kalpi. Some of these areas formed the kingdom of Lakshmi Bai, Rani of Jhansi, more than a century later. Chhattrasal also looked upon Baji Rao as his son and advised his own sons to join Baji Rao in every campaign in the vicinity of Bundelkhand and to look upon him as their blood brother.

The lion-hearted Chhattrasal died in December 1731 at the age of eighty-two. He left a number of sons, but his eldest two, Harde Sah and Jagat Raj, divided the remaining state between them, the former becoming the Raja of Panna and the latter, Raja of Jaitpur. The brothers always respected Baji Rao and fought alongside the Peshwa on a few subsequent occasions.

8

# The Bhatti Clan of Jaisalmer

The Golden Fort of Jaisalmer, with its hundred bastions, rising on a hillock deep in the Thar Desert, is one of the most spectacular sights in the country. Many years ago, before Jaisalmer had been discovered by tourists, I drove there on a cold winter morning from Jodhpur. The road is straight as an arrow and one can cover the 240 kilometres really fast. The only hazard and this was a long time ago, were the numerous bucks straying on the road from the surrounding scrub.

The Bhatti Rajputs of Jaisalmer traditionally trace their descent from Hare Krishna and are a branch of the Yadu race. Their own legends speak of a vast tide of Krishna's people, the Yadus, along with the Pandus migrating west of the Indus.

Over several centuries their route is traced from Indraprastha, Mathura, Prayag, Dwarka, Behera, Gujni (Ghazni in Afghanistan) and again on their expulsion from that area back to India at Shalivahanpur in the Punjab; from where a branch moved to Tannote in the Thar Desert and finally to Jaisalmer, which was founded in 1156. The latter part of the route unfolds the gradual peopling of the great Indian desert.

According to one tradition, one of these migratory branches moving in a more westerly direction even settled far from India in an alien land. According to this version, the land was Egypt—Who were the Pharaohs? What was their race? Perhaps I am being too fanciful!

This whole story of the tide of migration from India and final return by the above route is given by the Brahmin Sukhdharma of Mathura. He traces it over several centuries naming ancient kings and their numerous battles.

Interestingly many scattered facts and geographical distinctions seem to confirm the truth of Sukhdharma's story. His account of their encounters with Syrian and Bactrian (Khorasan) kings are confirmed by the Greeks, who record that Antiochus the Great, the Syrian king, was slain in these regions by an Indo-Scythian prince, who the Greeks call by the name Soobahu and his grandson Guj. Both were Yadu princes of Gujni who were involved in conflicts against the Bactrian kings. Greek sources again indicate that their descendants opposed Alexander in his progress down the Indus, and their capital Samanagiri, yet exists on the lower Indus. All this proves that interaction between Central Asia and India was unrestricted.

Thus having confirmation of Sukhdharma's chronicles and on the basis of Bhatti traditions and genealogical records, we take up this story. The date of these events is stated as *Samvat* 72 (AD 16), which is centuries before Islam was established in West Asia. At this time Raja Guj of the Yadu line was the ruler in Gujni. His guardian goddess ordered him to build a fort here and name it after himself. When the fort was nearing completion, Guj had tiding that the King of *Room* (Rajputs commonly

*The Golden Fort: A symbol of Rajasthan's glorious past*

applied this term to both Greece and Rome) and the King of Khorasan with powerful armies were advancing from the shores of the ocean towards his territories. Guj immediately summoned his allies and also sought council from the guardian goddess of his race. The drums were sounded, the army was alerted and the astrologers assigned the moment for marching.

Here I must reproduce an English rendering of Sukhdharma's powerful and stirring description of the battle.

> The combined armies of Khorasan and Room advanced like waves of the ocean, caparisons and chains clanked on the backs of elephants, while instruments of war resounded through the host. Elephants moved like walking mountains; the sky was black with clouds of dust and bright *helms* (helmets) reflected the rays of the sun. Four *kos* (13 kilometres) separated the hostile armies. Raja Guj and his chieftains performed their ablutions and keeping the *joginis* (unclean spirits of Rajput marital mythology, who feed on the slain) in their rear, advanced to the combat. Each host rushed on like famished tigers; the earth trembled; the heavens were overcast, nor was aught visible in the gloom but the radiant *helm*.
>
> War bells resounded; horses neighed; masses of men advanced on each other, like the dark rolling clouds of *Bhadoon*. Hissing sped the feathered dart; the lion roar of the warriors was re-echoed; the edge of the sword deluged the ground with blood; on both sides blows resounded on the crackling bones. Here was Guj Rae, there the Khorasanis and Scythians, as if Time had encountered his fellow. Mighty warriors strew the earth; heroes fell in the cause of their lords.
>
> The army of the Khorasanis fled; they left twenty-five thousand souls entangled in the net of destruction; they abandoned elephants and horses and even the throne. Seven thousand Hindus lay dead on the field. The drum of victory resounded, and the Yadu returned triumphant to his capital.

With this victory, Guj's power became firm and he extended his hold over the neighbouring tracts towards the west. He then summoned the King of Kashmir to his presence. The latter refused saying, 'The world will scoff if I attend the stirrup of another king without being worsted in fight.' Guj then invaded Kashmir and having won, he married the king's beautiful daughter. They had a son whom they named Shalivahan.

When the young prince Shalivahan was twelve years old, the King of Khorasan once again invaded Guj's kingdom. Raja Guj locked himself within the temple of the Goddess Culadevi. For several days he meditated before the goddess who appeared before him and revealed his destiny. She told him, 'Gujni will pass from your hands and you will fall in its defence. Your descendants will however return and will once again possess Gujni but they will not remain Hindus. Send your son Shalivahan to live among the Hindus of the east. You must sacrifice yourself for Gujni, but the greater reward will be yours.'

Having heard his fate, Guj sent Shalivahan and the royal family to India. He then marched out to meet his foe, the King of Khorasan. This desperate struggle lasted five *pehars* (each *pehar* is one-fourth of a day). Thousands were killed and both Raja Guj and the King of Khorasan were slain. The Khorasan army then laid siege to Gujni. It was defended valiantly for thirty days under the leadership of Guj's uncle, Sehdev. Finally the Yaduvanshis undertook the *saka* (the fight to the death) and Gujni was lost.

When this fatal news reached Shalivahan, he was overcome by grief and lay upon the ground and would not rise for twelve days. After mourning to his heart's content, he finally reached the Punjab, where he laid the foundations of a city

which he named Shalivahanpur. This is believed to be what is today known as Sialkot or some say, Lahore.

After he had conquered the whole region of the Punjab, Shalivahan married the Tuar princess of Delhi. He then determined to redeem Gujni and avenge his father's death. He crossed Attock, defeated the local king and regained Gujni. He returned to the Punjab, where he died, having ruled for thirty-four years.

One of his descendants, Chakito inherited Gujni. By this time 'barbarians' who were tribes from west and central Asia had settled in great numbers in and around the mountain kingdom and soon they held prominent positions in Chakito's court. The 'barbarian' nobles pleaded with him to accept their faith and offered to make him master of Baluch Bukhara. The Uzbeg king who ruled Bukhara had but one child—a daughter. Chakito married the princess to become the king of all the land from Baluchistan and Bukhara to the frontier of Hindustan. From him are descended the Chagitai tribe. This assertion that the Chagitais are descended from the Yadus is a curious, though not a surprising one. Prior to Islam, all these tribes, whether Indo-Scythic or Tatar, professed a faith which may be termed Hinduism.

But let us get back to the Bhattis. According to their chronicles, the next important development was the invasion of Shalivahanpur from the west. The Bhattis had to abandon the region and gradually their descendants moved south along the Indus. The next in the line who achieved prominence was their king, Kehur. He laid the foundations of a castle which he named Tunnote in honour of Tunno Devi or Mata. This was the first settlement in the desert of India and the date of this event is clearly established as AD 731. Tunnote is about 120 kilometres north-west of Jaisalmer.

We are now on the terra firma of Bhatti chronology and the earlier inaccuracy of the dates of events no longer applies. The chronicles of ancient times are based more on legends, but as we progress in time, there is greater historic fidelity of events.

From the year 731, when the fortress of Tunnote was erected by the Bhattis, down to 1474, a period of 743 years, it is a story of constant warfare. Sometimes it is Bhatti Rajputs against other Rajputs clans and at other times, it is Bhattis fighting the Muslim Baluchees, Langahs and others. This carries on; swords are drawn, battles are fought, there are gallant deeds and mighty words, there is plunder and perfidy.

We next come to Jesul, who thought it important to build his capital at a spot better adapted to defence. On a rocky ridge in his domain, Jesul met a Brahmin, whose solitary hermitage was next to the fountain of Brimsir. The Brahmin told Jesul the history of the triple-peaked hill which overlooked his hermitage. He said that in the *Treta yug* (Silver Age), an ascetic called Kak resided at this fountain and the rivulet that issued from the fountain was named Kaga after the ascetic. Arjun, one of the Pandus came to attend a great sacrifice with Krishna. On this occasion Krishna foretold that in some distant age, a descendant of his should erect a town on the rivulet and would raise a castle on the Tricula, the triple-peaked mount. While Krishna thus prophesied, it was observed by Arjun that the water was bad. Krishna smote the rock with his *chakra*, whereupon a sweet spring bubbled up and on its margin was inscribed the prophetic stanzas, which the Brahmin hermit Essul now pointed out to the Bhatti. 'O prince of Yadu-vansa! Come to this land and on the mountain's top erect a triangular castle.' Essul also foretold that the intended fortress would be sacked two and a half times and that rivers of blood would flow.

We have followed the Bhatti annals from the expulsion of the tribe from the Punjab and the establishment of Tunnote in the Indian desert in 731 to the foundation of Jaisalmer 425 years later. The events recorded are corroborated by numerous synchronisms in the annals of the other states of Rajasthan which confirm their authenticity. This period is full of incidents and it is interesting as a simple story of the gradual peopling of the Indian desert. We see tribes and cities disappearing; new races and new capitals taking their place.

9

# Maharaja Sir Pratap Singh of Jodhpur and Idar

My family, having lived and worked in the princely states for generations, it was seemly to include one of the maharajas into these vignettes. There were so many colourful characters among them that it was difficult to decide which one. Among them were enlightened rulers and profligate princes, saints and scoundrels, heroes and cowards, sadists and boors, charmers and eccentrics. Originally, the founders of the princely states were valiant warriors who had carved out their principalities at the point of the sword and retained them against predators by indomitable courage and sacrifice. But once the British took over and realised that they did not pose any danger to their rule, but were actually bulwarks of the empire, they pampered and petted the maharajas and provided them total security not only from external aggression but also from internal uprising. Thus the warrior kings were transformed into carpet knights and lost their earlier manliness and vigour. There were however some exceptions.

One of the most honourable exceptions was Maharaja Sir Pratap Singh, a soldier, swashbuckler, a man of natural valour and unlike his fellow royalty, a man of Spartan upbringing, who followed an extreme regimen of discipline. There are many wonderful stories of his courage, chivalry and, courtesy. His loyalty to the British Crown was almost a religion for him and I must add it was totally ridiculous. He fought in most of the British wars; in 1897 on the Afghanistan frontier, in 1899 in China during the Boxer Rebellion, and in France and Palestine in the First World War.

Pratap Singh was born in the Meharangarh Fort in 1845, the third son of Maharaja Takhat Singh of Jodhpur. Pratap Singh's formal status was quite unusual among the princes in that he was always honoured as a head of state though he was a ruler of a state for only nine years. The Rathore clan of Jodhpur is closely related to the Rathores of Idar, a smaller state on the border of Rajasthan, not very far from Baroda. When the Maharaja of Idar died without leaving an heir, there were several claimants to the throne who all appealed to the viceroy. Sir Pratap Singh appealed directly to Queen Victoria. He sent her a cable which simply read 'Idar is mine'. His magic with the British worked and he got it. Nine years later, however, Pratap Singh abdicated his throne in Idar to act as Regent of Jodhpur when his nephew, who was to be the next maharaja, was a minor. Pratap Singh could have continued as Maharaja of Idar and lived a life of ease but he felt it was his duty to return to Jodhpur. Acting as Regent on more than one occasion due to the premature deaths of two rulers, he guided the destiny of Jodhpur for twenty years. It may be remembered that maharajas and regents were absolute rulers.

Before I pursue the military and sporting exploits of Sir Pratap, a few words on the princely states may be appropriate. In undivided India, these states comprised a little under half the subcontinent. A map of the time will show that there is almost contiguous state territory from the area bordering Central Asia to Kanyakumari, the southernmost point of the Indian peninsula. Thus one could travel the length of India, all 3,200 kilometres, without touching British India.

The 565 Indian states enjoyed varying degrees of autonomy depending on their size and importance. Broadly, the princely states fell into three categories. First were the ancient states which could trace their ancestry a thousand years or more. These included the Rajput states of Rajasthan, Central India and Saurashtra. The southern states of Mysore and Travancore also fell into the ancient category. Benjamin Disraeli, the distinguished prime minister, said in the British Parliament in 1876, 'Some Indian princes sat on thrones which were in being when England was a Roman colony.'

The second group of states was established in the chaos following the fragmentation of the Mughal Empire in the 1700s—Hyderabad, Rampur etc. In the third group of principalities fell those that were carved out by military adventurers at the point of the sword. These included the Maratha, Jat and Sikh states. Of these the important ones were the Maratha states of Gwalior, Baroda and Holkar, the Jat state of Bharatpur and the Sikh states of the Punjab, notably Patiala. The Muslim states of Bhopal and Bahawalpur also fell in this category.

Of the 565 states, there were 118 Salute states that had full powers of internal autonomy and they could make their own laws and had powers of life and death over their subjects. As you went down the state scale in terms of size and importance, there was greater British control over general administration. The states varied in size from Hyderabad and Jammu and Kashmir, which were the size of France to the absurdly small states which were less than 15 square kilometres in size. However 'the states were not British territory and their subjects were not British subjects'.

*Meharangarh Fort*

*Maharaja Sir Pratap Singh*

Returning however to Maharaja Pratap Singh, it is recorded that even as a child, he was absolutely fearless to the point of foolhardiness. At the age of five, he caught hold of a big monkey, which had been threatening his little friends and both fell off a high wall. A year later, he dared to jump off a tree, he did so instantly and broke both legs. He had a limp for the rest of his life. It did not bother him however as he spent most of his time on horseback. At seven, he was an expert horseman. When he was nine, he asked his father for a shotgun, which was refused. He managed to get hold of one of his father's rifles and shot partridges with it. Consequently he became an expert marksman. It is recorded that at the same age 'he tried to dispatch his first leopard with his sword, but while drawing it, he realised that the beast was about to leap and brought up his rifle instead. The leopard obligingly seized the barrel in his jaws and the boy blew off the back of his head.'

Two sports at which he excelled were pig-sticking and polo. Both sports require skilled horsemanship, strength and guts. Galloping at breakneck speed on a grassy, uneven and bouldered surface after a fast disappearing wild boar was exhilarating. It was also dangerous. A wild boar has sharp tusks and it is quick and ferocious in attack. Every charge it makes may leave a wound in the horse or the rider. You have to kill the beast with a strong spear thrust riding at full tilt.

Sir Frederick Roberts, commander-in-chief in India, was once out pig-sticking with Sir Pratap. Sir Frederick was a small man and not skilled at this sport. He speared a pig in the belly, but the ferocious animal turned and ripped open the underparts of Sir Frederick's horse, throwing him out of the saddle. Sir Pratap dismounted instantly and took the boar by the hind legs, until Sir Frederick could collect himself and finally spear the animal to death. They were lifelong friends after this and fought together in several wars.

On another occasion in 1921, the Prince of Wales went out pig-sticking with Pratap Singh in Jodhpur. When the future King Edward VIII in the middle of the action dismounted from his horse which left him exposed, the seventy-seven year old Rajput rebuked him saying, 'I know you are the Prince of Wales and you know you are the Prince of Wales but the pig does not know you are the Prince of Wales!'

But above all Sir Pratap was a soldier, one who was devoted to the service of the British Crown. We have spoken about his fearlessness. One of the Viceroys, Lord Hardinge, wrote in his book *My Indian Years, 1910-16*, 'The Maharaja of Idar and sometime Regent of Jodhpur, Sir Pratap Singh comes from warrior stock. His courage was extraordinary and he did not know what fear meant. He excelled as the best pig-sticker in India, but he had been trained to fight a boar on foot with only a knife in his hand ... He was of Spartan simplicity ...'. And Hardinge here added an asinine comment, 'a truly White man among Indians.'

The first military action Sir Pratap was involved in was when a brother, ambitious but ill advised, seized a fortress some distance from the capital Jodhpur and declared himself independent of the maharaja. The state only had a token army but Pratap Singh rallied troops belonging to loyal noblemen. They were untrained and did not even have uniforms. Pratap ordered saffron coloured uniforms for them and led the action. The rebel seeing the saffron clothed men that traditionally means 'victory or death', felt that things were getting out of hand and immediately gave up the idea and surrendered to his brother.

In 1889, the Government of India, prompted by Sir Frederick Roberts, suggested that Jodhpur State raise two regiments of cavalry, foot and artillery for imperial service outside the state when needed in an imperial cause. The Jodhpur Lancers, under Sir Pratap Singh proved to be crack troops. Sir Frederick looked them over and declared that 'the grand tradition of the Rajput race will be most carefully respected when the time comes for them to take their place in the field with the troops of the Queen Empress of India.' The Jodhpur Lancers were also called the 'Sardar Risala'. Interestingly their memory is preserved by the last horsed regiment, in the present day Indian Army, the 61st Cavalry headquartered at Jaipur, an elegant and brave body of men. The cutlery of the 61st Cavalry still bears the crest of the Sardar Risala.

In 1899, Sir Pratap took a regiment of the Jodhpur Lancers to China to help put down the Boxer Rebellion. They encamped near the Great Wall, not far from a regiment of Cossacks. Sir Pratap declared that 'the Cossacks were interesting but inferior!' In the first action, the Lancers charged the unfortunate Boxers but curiously they used the blunt end of their lances until they were sure that Sir Pratap had drawn first blood.

Sir Pratap often stated that 'war is an open door to heaven' and just as he had hoped, the Sardar Risala was ordered in 1914 to fight in the First World War. Sir Pratap was now nudging seventy years of age but he swore 'he would kill Germans and die for his King Emperor'. The Jodhpur Lancers sailed from Bombay with orders for the defence of the Suez Canal. But Sir Pratap refused to disembark his troops in Egypt because there were no Germans there. Sir Frederick was now Field Marshall Earl Roberts of Kandahar. Sir Pratap was also friends with many other British generals and after some parlaying within this network; Sir Pratap Singh managed to get the Lancers to Marseilles and asked to head for Flanders where the fighting was at its fiercest. Here Field Marshall Frederick Roberts came to see the Jodhpur Lancers and meet his old friend Pratap but the harsh winter cold got him and he died in their midst of pneumonia. Sir Pratap accompanied his body all the way to London for a state funeral.

The Sardar Risala stayed on the battlefield for over three years, but it was mostly digging trenches and drilling with only one action where they fought as infantry. Pratap Singh still seeking glory or death asked every general, 'When will you order the Jodhpur Lancers to a cavalry charge?' He usually got the answer that it would happen soon. Pratap then approached the Commander-in-Chief Haig, who he had known since their polo playing days when Haig was a captain posted in Delhi and Secunderabad, and asked him the same question. Later Pratap wrote, 'One day

*Sir Pratap Singh leading the Jodhpur Lancers through a French village*

Haig told me, the time was not quite right. Whichever of the two antagonists will make undue haste will suffer defeat. But when the time comes we will order the Lancers to charge.' The time apparently came in November 1917 at a place called Cambria. After three years of attrition, the British tanks had broken through the 'German trenches,but the tanks were stopped by a canal. It was then that the cavalry was brought up for the promised charge, but they were also stopped by the same canal.' This was a great piece of luck, for hidden beyond the canal were hundreds of machine guns of the German support line.

Early in 1918, the Sardar Risala was shipped to Palestine to fight the Turks. In July 1918, they were in the Jordan Valley which, at the time, was a hellhole of disease, infection and insanitation. Engaging the enemy in an encounter, the Lancers at one point briefly fell back; Pratap Singh gave a simple order to his troops, 'You can go forward

The Mirror *showing Sir Pratap Singh with his son and a rajah in Flanders*

and be killed by the enemy's bullets or you can fall back and be executed by me.' Later that month the Lancers received the long awaited order. Sir Pratap, all of seventy-four years of age, along with two squadrons charged at last and broke the Turkish line. Pratap stayed in the saddle for over thirty hours except for a four hour break, because, dismounting was too painful for his broken and twisted legs.

Pratap unfortunately missed the Sardar Risala's finest hour when they took the town of Haifa at the gallop, lancing any Turk bold enough to face them and rounding up 700 Turkish prisoners. Just before this operation, Pratap Singh had been summoned to Jodhpur to once again act as Regent, as another young maharaja had died suddenly. He therefore missed Haifa. In this action, Pratap lost Major Dalpat Singh, the son of his closest and oldest friend, who only with his trumpet major beside him, galloped at a machine gun, killed all the gunners, captured the gun and the Turkish commander, thus winning the Military Cross. When the British general telegraphed the news of Dalpat Singh's action and death to Sir Pratap, he replied saying, 'Dalpat's greatest day has arrived'. Death and glory were embedded in his heart. By the time of the Armistice, the Jodhpur Lancers had eighty-eight awards for valour, including a Military Cross for Sir Pratap's own son.

I have also come across references of Sir Pratap having fought in the 1890s on the Afghan frontier when he was young man. However, details were not available and I leave it at that.

Needless to say all his actions since he was a young man had made Pratap Singh a darling of the British. His gallantry and old world charm won him many admirers in that country, including the royal family. Several years before the World War, Sir Pratap, as he was known there, was formally invited to attend Queen Victoria's Golden Jubilee celebrations. Most of the rulers at that time used to stay at the Savoy or Claridges or one of the top notch hotels of London but Sir Pratap, when he arrived, said he would stay at Buckingham Palace. He was politely informed that Her Majesty had not invited him to stay at Buckingham Palace, to which he apparently replied, 'Suppose I were to invite Her Majesty to Jodhpur, I would never expect her to stay at a hotel or someone else's house. She would stay in my palace. So obviously Her Majesty will not expect me to stay at a hotel or elsewhere.' Where upon he promptly marched into the palace.

On another occasion, in 1887 to be exact, many of the maharajas had assembled at the court to be presented to Queen Victoria. They had come with *nazar* (formal gifts). Sir Pratap realising that he had brought nothing, improvised by taking out the diamond *kalgi* (ornament in headgear) from his turban and presented it to her. When she extended her hand for the customary kiss, he put it across his eyes, explaining that it was to signify the surrender of a warrior's greatest treasure—his sight. This ready gallantry made its mark.

On this visit to England, some of his baggage had been lost en route on the ship which led to last minute tailoring. He introduced the Jodhpur breeches to London when he had to explain to a tailor how to cut them. Soon these breeches became the rage in that country.

*Interior of Meharangarh Fort*

Pratap was not only high profile but also upstaged most people, including viceroys. He welcomed and guarded all three Princes of Wales on their Indian tours and could claim the friendship of Queen Victoria, Edward VIII and George V. In those days all this would have been important. In India, Lord Curzon made him Commandant of the Imperial Cadets Corps, which was planned to instill some discipline and military virtues into the sons of ruling princes. Sir Pratap designed its white uniform with sky blue and gold facing. He was a strict taskmaster and suggested that the annual vacation should be abolished as during these vacations the young men sank into luxury and ease and this would undo all the Spartan training and discipline they had been put through.

At one stage of his life, Pratap Singh, although not overly religious, came under the influence of Swami Dayanand Saraswati, the founder of the Arya Samaj. But before he embraced the sect, he had to be doubly reassured that he would not have to give up eating meat. Rajputs are great carnivores and when he was told that this would not interfere with his cuisine, in relief he commented, 'In the history of the world there is not a single instance to show that any vegetarian community ever became brave or warlike!'

Sir Pratap's excessive loyalty to the British Crown sometimes made him the butt of jokes in India. One amusing anecdote I heard about him when I was a young boy is worth recounting. *Shikar* (hunting) was a favourite sport in the princely states; it was almost a substitute for war. It was always pursued in great style; Rolls Royces on jungle paths, elaborate carpeted tents for living and entertaining, well stocked bars and so on. I cannot quite remember where this shoot took place, but there were many maharajas including Pratap Singh as guests. Pratap's bathroom tent was very well furnished with all essentials including an elaborate 'thunderbox' with a velvet upholstered seat for his comfort. There was only one major problem with it. Every time Sir Pratap took his seat, the thunderbox resounded loudly to the sounds of the British National Anthem *God Save the King*. Sir Pratap had no option but to spring up and stand to attention. It happened every time he sat and finally he decided to go 'jungling' in the tall grass!

One night in 1920, Pratap Singh was taken very ill and he knew that death was close. He dressed himself in his finest military uniform and sat ramrod straight in a carved silver chair, with his beautifully embellished *khanda* (sword) in his hand to fight his last battle. He sat through the night and apparently drove his adversary away for he was fine the next morning. Two years later, in September 1922, the adversary did return and caught him unawares.

*Handprints on the walls by the women commiting sati*

The biggest expression of wifely devotion to a dead husband is sati, the act of self-immolation where a widow joins a late husband on the funeral pyre. When the grandson of Sir Pratap, Brigadier Jabbar Singh of the Jodhpur Lancers died, his wife Sugankunverba dressed herself in fine wedding clothes, wore ivory bangles and climbed the funeral pyre and became a sati. This was in 1950 and the last recorded instance of a royal sati. She is worshipped to this day.

# 10

# Maratha Admiral–Kanhoji Angre

A boy called Angre was at school with me. His father was one of the notable Sardars of Gwalior State. He was a pleasant enough chap but a bit of a bore about one of his ancestors, Kanhoji Angre, who he said, 'had beaten the pants off the British and the Portuguese' about 200 years earlier. I did not pay attention to his stories till I learnt more about Kanhoji Angre during a history lesson. I have come across many more facts about this fascinating character since then.

In the early eighteenth century, a long bitter war was going on between the Mughals and the Marathas. The European traders, mainly the Portuguese and the English, who had established toeholds on the west coast, watched from the sidelines and minded their businesses and prospered. The conflicting giants, the Mughals and the Marathas, hardly took any notice of these obsequious traders. Had the Portuguese and the English been asked to name an enemy, they would of course have mentioned each other but the man uppermost in their minds would have been Kanhoji Angre, the man they chose to call a pirate. Over several years Angre carried on a running land and sea battle against these European powers.

*Portuguese map of India, 1630*

Kanhoji Angre's origins are obscure but it is widely believed that he was born around 1670 in a Maratha-Kshatriya family in a village near Pune. There were no schools then but thanks to a Brahmin of the village, who took an interest in the boy, Angre got a good education and turned out to be a surprisingly learned man, which was most unusual among the contemporary Maratha warrior class. But then he was an unusual man.

'A sailor and a soldier equally fond of ships and horses, a powerful swimmer and dashing horseman... '

He was an excellent swordsman as well as a diplomat of uncommon ability, clever at advocating his side of the case. He had three wives but there were many more women in his life. In contrast to this streak of riotous living and loving, he was an intensively religious man. He had a blind veneration for a godman called Brahmendra Swami (who was not very different from the godmen of today—a mixture of a fabulously rich businessman, so called saint and a religious preceptor).

In physical appearance, Kanhoji was a man of middle height, but strong as an ox and 'exuded a hairy-chested maleness'. He had arrogant piercing eyes and a brown skin burnt to a darker hue by the sun and the sea. 'In warfare he found a complete, exultant fulfillment of life.'

The foundation of the Maratha navy was laid by Shivaji. Once in possession of the Konkan Coast, he realised the advantages of a strong fighting fleet. Shivaji had only a modest number of fighting vessels but he developed strong coastal forts. In artillery and navigation, however, the Marathas were no match for the Europeans and still had much to learn from them.

*Kanhoji Angre*

About this time, the Portuguese had effectively established their sovereignty on the sea. They, therefore, insisted that merchant ships, Indian or foreign, would be permitted on the water only if they purchased the Portuguese 'cartaz'. Without this the ships had to pay a high penalty or at times be sunk. This brought the Portuguese much profit.

When Kanhoji Angre succeeded to the Chief Command of the Maratha navy, it had already been in existence for forty years. Angre's brief, as mentioned earlier, was to protect Maratha merchant men from the *firangees* and *hubshies* (Europeans and Abyssinians, respectively). In order to do this and to secure the sovereignty of the sea, the fleet had to be expanded. Money was needed for additional ships and enlisting more men. The only way to raise money was by compelling alien traders to purchase Angre's 'cartaz' and he started his own permits known as *dastaks* on the same lines as the Portuguese. This immediately brought him into conflict with the Portuguese who had profitably held this monopoly so far.

The accompanying map shows 800 kilometres of coastline from Surat to Karwar and also shows the overall situation around the year 1700. Surat was a Mughal provincial headquarter but the English had a factory there. Bassein, with its strong fortress and the environs including Thana, was Portuguese. The island of Bombay belonged to the East India Company and it had grown into a big city of 70,000 inhabitants, but it was totally dependent on the surrounding countryside, which was a Maratha territory, for its supplies. Sixteen kilometres further south was the Maratha island of Khanderi. Kolaba, 30 kilometres further down, was Kanhoji Angre's headquarters. Chaul was Portuguese, while a few miles south of this were the impregnable island fortress of Janjira which belonged to the Siddis,

with a small pocket of land around it. From Janjira to Goa, the coastline was controlled and administered by the Marathas. Goa, a segment about 80 kilometres long and 50 kilometres at its widest, was a strongly garrisoned, well-fortified Portuguese enclave.

In 1703, Kanhoji Angre informed the East India Company that he would seize all their ships which did not carry his *dastaks*. Soon after this, he seems to have made good this threat. According to the Surat Records of the English, he captured several of their ships, 'including the *Diamond of Madras* which was carrying 12 guns and 26 European personnel, her cargo worth near two lakhs of rupees.'

We do not know when exactly Angre first challenged the Portuguese supremacy of the seas but his first victim was a Portuguese *pal*-of-war (sea-going vessel), richly laden and carrying on board the retired Governor of Chaul, who ultimately died from the rigours of his imprisonment. Angre then captured several other ships and took many Portuguese prisoners. The richest Portuguese spoil Angre obtained was in 1712 when he boldly attacked the merchant fleet sailing from Goa to the Portuguese ports further north. The fleet was convoyed by two frigates under the command of Luiz da Costa. Kanhoji attacked the frigates with his pals, dismantled the Portuguese flagship and captured the entire merchant fleet. This was a great calamity for the Portuguese, for the yearly Armada was the most important trading enterprise of the merchants of Goa and carried the fortune of many of its citizens.

The Portuguese also found that their other possessions on the coast had been cut off from Goa and Angre was in a position to dislocate their communications both by land and by sea. Finally, the viceroy resolved to take offence and sent a strong flotilla to reduce Kolaba, Angre's stronghold. Angre was reluctant to hazard a naval battle. He responded by hauling his fleet ashore on to dry land, well out of range of the Portuguese guns. This was a drill he carried out at the beginning of every monsoon to save the ships from the fury of the elements.

The Portuguese captain was totally nonplussed by Kanhoji's ludicrous stratagem of pulling his fleet out of range of his powerful guns. Neither could he take his fleet too close to the shore as Angre's shore guns would have made mincemeat out of his ships. The Portuguese captain however continued his blockade and the Siddis also arrived with their ships to help, but the blockade was totally ineffectual as Angre got his supplies by land. Finally, after three months they both gave up and departed.

Over the years, almost the entire coast from Goa to Bombay remained in Angre's hands. Using considerable foresight he strengthened the fortifications of both his ports and land forts. On the coast every creek, harbour and river mouth was converted into a stronghold. He also established shipyards and employed foreign experts to build his new ships.

Apart from the Portuguese, Kanhoji continued clashing with English ships and more often than not his attack was successful. In 1707, he captured the Company's ship *Monsoon* and sank the frigate *Bombay*. The Company complained to the directors that Kanhoji Angre 'can take any ship, except the largest European ships, along the coast from Surat to Dabul; he takes all private merchants he meets.'

Manohar Malgaonkar in his book *The Sea Hawk* says that Angre employed special tactics against superior ships and superior arms. He devised a kind of guerilla warfare of the sea. 'When the European ships came close to the coast they had to reduce sail and slow down. This was the time when Angre's ships hiding in some convenient cove would emerge and swoop down upon them. He also tried to compensate for his inferior guns by keeping his ships within range of his coastal guns.'

Malgaonkar goes on to say that Angre endeavoured to keep astern of their quarry with the object of keeping out of the way of broadsides. His objective was not so much to sink an enemy ship as to slow it down so that he could board her. With this in mind, his *ghurabs* and *gallivats* (different types of fighting ships), while keeping astern would fire at the rigging of his victims so that they perforce had to slow down. 'Once his men had closed in, their victim was doomed, for a hand-to-hand combat, in the use of the sword and the shield; the Marathas were far superior to the European sailors and soldiers.' Angre also took advantage of the fact that he could send many more men into the attack than his victims could carry on board.

In 1712, Angre captured two more of the East India Company's ships; one, the governor's own yacht and another, an English vessel *Anne*. Both these ships were escorted by a frigate *Defiance* which carried fourteen guns. The English ships were attacked by Angre's *ghurabs* while they were still in sight of the island of Bombay. The armed escort *Defiance* made a cowardly escape and fled back to the harbour. As all this happened in full view of Bombay, it caused great consternation. The captain of *Defiance* was immediately dismissed from service.

Angre had, however, taken on three enemies at the same time the Portuguese, the English and the Siddis. He realised the folly of this and tried to make peace with the English. At the same time, his close links with the peshwa secured Angre against any invasion from the mainland as the peshwa promised help in such an eventuality. This effectively removed any threat from the Siddis who, despite having lost some territory to Angre, withdrew from the struggle against him.

In 1715, Charles Boone was appointed the governor of Bombay. Boone fancied himself as something of a military genius, but on assessing the military situation he decided that they were not in a good posture to oppose Angre, and consequently Boone started to make military preparations. The first thing he did was to build a

wall around Bombay at great expense and mount on it 48-pounder guns. This wall with its six or seven gates, which have given their names to so many of Bombay's streets (Church Gate, Bazaar Gate and others), was meant to protect Bombay against Kanhoji Angre.

Boone also launched a drive to build more fighting ships. He had constructed at Surat, four large frigates—each of them carrying a large number of heavy guns and various other civil and naval vessels. Within two years, the new Governor Boone had built up a fleet of modern ships more powerful in firepower, if not in actual numbers, than the fleet of the Marathas.

In April 1716, Boone sent his ships to attack Vengurla, one of Angre's ports. It is not clear why Vengurla was chosen as a target as it was of no great importance. For two days *Fame*, *Britannia* and *Revenge* bombarded Vengurla. But when the English landing party was just about to go into the attack, there was a furious quarrel

*A British-commanded Indo-Portuguese naval force attacks the fort of Geriah, 1756*

between Weekes, the commander of the navy, and Stanton, the commander of the landing party. The reason for the quarrel is not known, but it led to the abandonment of the Vengurla expedition. The flotilla returned to Bombay without achieving a thing. Governor Boone was disgusted and sacked the navy Commander, Weekes.

Boone's next foray was more significant as he ordered his fleet to make an attack on Vijaydurg, also known as Gheria. This attack was aimed not only at capturing the coastal port but was also an attempt to destroy a large part of Angre's fleet as it lay at anchorage just before the monsoon.

Vijaydurg was twelve hours sail from Bombay and in command was Captain Berlew. His plan, fully endorsed by Boone, was to smash the fortifications by an intense cannonade from his frigates and then send a lighted fireship, amidst Angre's *ghurabs*, *gallivats* and *pals* all huddled together and roofed with inflammable palm leaves. Once the fireship was in their midst, the pre-monsoon winds would send up the lot in flames. After this masterstroke a strong landing party would go ashore, destroy the garrison and take Vijaydurg by escalade or climbing the fort walls with the help of ladders. It may be stated that Governor Boone had sent a very strong force consisting of over 2,000 well trained men, while the Maratha garrison in Vijaydurg did not exceed 100 and Kanhoji Angre was not there. The plan of the English was an excellent one. Boone had checked and double checked and pronounced it perfect.

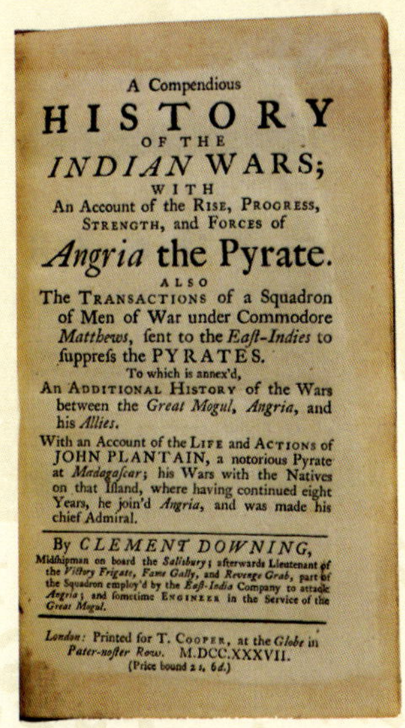
A Compendious
HISTORY
OF THE
*INDIAN* WARS;
WITH
An Account of the RISE, PROGRESS, STRENGTH, and FORCES of
*Angria* the Pyrate.
ALSO
The TRANSACTIONS of a Squadron of Men of War under Commodore *Matthews*, ſent to the *Eaſt-Indies* to ſuppreſs the PYRATES.
To which is annex'd,
An ADDITIONAL HISTORY of the Wars between the *Great Mogul*, *Angria*, and his *Allies*.
With an Account of the LIFE and ACTIONS of JOHN PLANTAIN, a notorious Pyrate at *Madagaſcar*; his Wars with the Natives on that Iſland, where having continued eight Years, he join'd *Angria*, and was made his chief Admiral.

By *CLEMENT DOWNING*,
Midſhipman on board the *Salisbury*; afterwards Lieutenant of the *Victory Frigate*, *Fame Gally*, and *Revenge Grab*, part of the Squadron employ'd by the *Eaſt-India* Company to attack *Angria*; and ſometime ENGINEER in the Service of the *Great Mogul*.

*London*: Printed for T. COOPER, at the *Globe* in *Pater-noſter Row*. M.DCC.XXXVII.
(Price bound 2 s. 6 d.)

Clement Downing, one of the sailors with a literary bent of mind, wrote an account of this and subsequent English expeditions entitled *A compendious history of the Indian Wars ... forces of Angria the Pyrate*. According to Downing, the English fleet sailed into Vijaydurg harbour and upon lining up started an intense bombardment, firing the cannons as fast as the barrels could be cooled. This went on for two days and the attackers felt that the Indians would, at any moment, come out with a flag of truce. However, the strong fortifications held up well against the heavy guns of the frigates. The shells that fell inside the fortress did little damage because their fuses were too long or had fallen on rocks. The landing party, which was to follow the cannonade, proclaimed that the shore was too rocky to land and thus could do little. To make matters worse, when the English tried to escalade, they encountered a major problem: the walls of the fort were too high and their scaling ladders too short. In this attempt a number of them were killed and wounded. The final calamity occurred when they resorted to their most effective stratagem, their secret fireship; they discovered, to their utter horror, that the defenders had erected a strong boom across the entrance channel, which stopped the fireship. This elementary precaution taken by the Marathas came as a total surprise to the English. The Maratha garrison, far from retreating, jeered and taunted the enemy from the secure shelter of the walls.

When night fell, all that the English had achieved was knocking down three houses inside Vijaydurg. It was clear that they would not be able to take the place, so they abandoned the attempt. But typically the Bombay records state: 'Returned our ships having destroyed one town of Angrais.'

Boone's zeal had been somewhat dampened by the failure of two of his expeditions against Angre. He therefore attempted nothing more until November 1718, by which time more help had arrived from England: more soldiers and first line ships. This time Boone was determined that nothing must go wrong. The third attack was to be made against the Maratha island of Khanderi which lay ten miles south of Bombay and three miles from the coast. For this venture, Boone assembled twenty-one first line ships, each of which had two or more *gallivats* as their permanent auxiliary vessels. Thus the total number of assorted vessels added up to more than fifty. The ships between them carried over 200 guns. The total manpower of this formidable force numbered between 2,500 and 3,000 men.

Unfortunately Boone chose for his Admiral, not one of his own English captains, but a Portuguese named Manuel de Castro, a wandering soldier of fortune, who had recently been in the service of Angre. Later, to escape Angre's wrath, he had fled to Bombay. He had crept into the good graces of Boone by assuring him that he knew every nook and corner of Angre's ports as well as the disposition of his fortifications. This appointment as Admiral, not unnaturally, caused a lot of annoyance among the Company's captains and Boone finally had to give in. Manuel de Castro's command was reduced to that of a few *gallivats*. Boone then decided to take command of the expedition himself and proceeded to hoist his flag on board the *Addison*.

This formidable fleet anchored near Khanderi on 3 November 1718. The Marathas had never seen so many ships assembled together and they were suitably impressed. Kanhoji Angre incidentally was not in Khanderi at the time but had a very able deputy-in-command there. After the island had been reconnoitered for a landing place, the English ships were ordered to open fire, which continued the whole day. The Maratha garrison replied vigorously till the early evening, when their ammunition ran out.

On 4 November, again an uninterrupted cannonade was kept up from first light to dusk. There was however, no answering fire from the fort guns throughout the day. This confirmed the impression that the defenders' ammunition had indeed run out, and the British were full of hope that the fort could not resist a determined assault. Boone told de Castro to lie at the entrance to the harbour of Khanderi and not let any supplies reach the island from outside, under any circumstances.

But according to the writer-sailor Clement Downing, to whom we have referred earlier, Manuel de Castro proved 'not only incompetent but treacherous'. During the night he is said to have landed on the island, disclosed Boone's plan of attack and let five Maratha ships with ammunition and supplies pass through his *gallivats* and into the harbour.

The landing by the foreigners was scheduled for 5 November, and as the time for this drew near, the English ships moved into their allotted positions and resumed shelling of the fort to provide covering fire for the assaulting parties, who approached the fort in boats. It was however found that the tide was too high; this caused major problems for the boats. Before the English were able to get on ashore, they encountered heavy small arms fire and the Indians shot down sixty of them. The English then gave up the assault and fled back to their ships.

To add to the confusion and astonishment of the attackers, the Maratha cannons for which ammunition had been received during the night, started firing again. The English ships had been brought in close to the island under the illusion that the ammunition of the defenders was exhausted; consequently the Maratha cannons firing at a brisk rate caused heavy damage to the English fleet.

The second attempt at landing was scheduled for the next day. As the landing party boats made for the shore, they encountered heavy fire from the fort's guns. To make matters worse, the current was too strong and caused some of the boats to capsize. Nevertheless, despite these setbacks, the landing party persevered until it reached one of the outer gates of the fort.

Here Gideon Russell, who was leading the volunteers, was killed, and the command of the landing party devolved on our literacy fount Clement Downing and a certain Mr Steele who with axe in his hand, along with the other soldiers, tried to cut down the bars on the wooden gate and failed.

But two captains, whose names are not mentioned, disgraced themselves. One captain threw down his sword in abject fear and fled. The other captain marched up to the gate and fired his pistol into the lock, trying to burst it open. As he might have anticipated, the bullet rebounded and struck him in the nose. The pain in the wound overcame his courage and sounding a retreat, all the soldiers including their Commander, Major Stanton, fled back to their boats.

Clement Downing writes that a small party under him still persevered but the Indians shot them down from the walls. At this stage, the small Maratha garrison inside the fort counter-attacked; they emerged from the fort and fell on the broken enemy and put them to the sword. A few survivors, including the fortunate Downing, finally reached the safety of their boats.

Charles Boone was justly angered at this third failure. In Bombay he held a parade where the captain who had thrown his sword and cut and run from the gate was publicly dismissed and his 'sword was broken'. Obviously it had later been retrieved by someone. De Castro was court-martialled and sent as a slave to the island of St Helena. From there, however, he managed to escape and return to India where he is supposed to have rejoined Angre.

Boone, having punished those responsible for the defeat and with his zeal still intact, prepared for a fourth expedition. Malgaonkar has a hilarious description of this venture in his book *The Sea Hawk*. Boone, this time constructed a floating vessel which he named *The Phram*. This was described as a floating castle or a machine that would be almost cannon-proof. It had a low draught, as it had a flat platform for a floor and its sides were very strongly built. It was fitted with a mast carrying a top sail and it had 12 heavy guns, each a 48-pounder. It was believed that if towed close to its target, it would be able to batter down any fortification while sustaining little damage to itself. The fact however was *The Phram* was very poorly designed.

After his earlier failure against Vijaydurg, Boone decided to once again attack Angre's stronghold. It would be tedious to follow this attack in detail except to recount the farcical story of *The Phram*, the floating castle. When the fleet arrived at Vijaydurg, the captain immediately ordered *The Phram* to open fire. However, all her shots fell into the water barely twenty yards away. It was found that her gun slits were cut too low into her sides and the gun carriages were so high that no shot could be fired without depressing the barrels to the lowest. The alteration involved enlarging the gun slits by chopping down parts of her cannon proof walls. All the fleet's carpenters were kept busy the whole day till it was fit for action.

Lieutenant Wise was the commander of *The Phram* but either he had no idea of gunnery or the vessel was so woefully designed that it was a matter of pure luck that firing from this contraption did not sink one of the Company's own ships. The English Captain now ordered *The Phram* to sneak in closer. To raise the flagging spirits of his men, the Captain sent twelve dozen bottles of wine and arrack which was a disastrous plan.

When the time came for *The Phram* to fire her first salvo, Lieutenant Wise was too drunk to take any part in the action. However a handful of sailors, who were surprisingly still sober, now decided to try their hand at gunnery, but each in his own way. One of *The Phram*'s guns burst and another whether through carelessness or bad workmanship, it will never be known, fired a shot on the opposite side and into a boat full of African soldiers waiting to make a landing. According to one of the ship's logbook, 'The poor wretches were terribly scorched and injured'. Meanwhile, the Indians were firing back vigorously from Vijaydurg Fort and two of their shots fell inside *The Phram*, killing fifteen men and wounding thirty others.

By nightfall, the English Captain had had enough and taking advantage of a light breeze, he decided to withdraw all his ships. On their return journey they fell in with two pirate ships, whom they could easily have overpowered, but the Captain was so alarmed that he burnt *The Phram* as it was slowing down the rest of the fleet, and sailed back to the Bombay harbour as fast as he could turning the whole episode farcical beyond belief.

The success that Angre had chalked up finally led the Court of Directors of the East India Company to appeal to the British government for assistance in their military operations. In 1722, the government decided to send out a squadron of four men-of-war under the command of Commodore Matthews. Boone was delighted with this development. The whole of Bombay turned out to welcome the British Navy. The four fine ships gathered in the great harbour, but it was days before Commodore Matthews agreed to land. He demanded the ceremonial welcome due to him and refused to go ashore at Bombay until he had received a salute from the shore batteries. As a highly placed officer of the Royal Navy, he deemed himself superior in rank to Boone, the governor of Bombay and president of the Council, and would not leave his ship until the city fired a salute in his honour. On the other hand, Boone as President of the Council was the British King's representative and considered himself senior to the commodore.

*Kolaba cannons*

After much controversy and many messages being sent to and fro, Boone lost the battle of gun salutes. He arranged for a salute to be fired for Matthews, following

which the commodore and his officers landed. The naval officers, however, bore themselves in a very superior manner leaving no doubt of the poor opinion they had of the Company officials. The latter, although humiliated by the arrogance of the naval personnel, still hoped for great things from their quarrelsome disposition and fancied that the mere sight of one of Angre's fortresses would arouse them to such fury that resistance would be impossible.

Commodore Matthews and Boone patched up their differences and discussed various plans of action. Finally, it was resolved to make an alliance with their traditional enemies, the Portuguese. This would have been the obvious course against their common Indian enemy but mutual suspicion had so long stood in the way. Messengers were sent to both the Portuguese Viceroy at Goa and to the 'General of the North' as the Portuguese Governor of Bassein and the island of Salsette were called. An enticing vision was conjured of the whole area of the Konkan divided between the Portuguese and the English. The strong hold of Kolaba was to be awarded to the Portuguese and Vijaydurg to the English. The desire for conquest and territory, which perforce had been subdued, was now rekindled. Greed enables bitter enemies to become allies.

Both the General of the North, Don António de Mello e Castro and the Viceroy, Don Francisco José de Sampaio, came to Bombay and keeping aside their old enmity with the English, signed a treaty in August 1721. Kolaba, the headquarters of Angre, was chosen for this momentous operation. Both the high Portuguese officials agreed

*Kolaba Fort*

to lead contingents from Goa and Bassein in person. Boone entertained them lavishly and they, in turn, consented courteously to serve under a British Commander. Boone, however, repeated his earlier folly and appointed Robert Cowan, one of his Council, as general. He also distributed a number of military commissions among other civil servants of the Company.

Parasnis and Kincaid, the eminent historians of the Marathas, state that 'the allied forces numbered no less than 5,000 men with 24 cannons, and if properly led, should have conquered all Angre's possessions. But the General-in-Chief, Cowan, had no experience of war. Commodore Matthews had only seen service at sea and not on land and between the English and the Portuguese was a mutual distrust born of more than a century of rivalry and warfare'. The English force went through three months of intensive training and was finally pronounced fit for action. Boone reviewed the troops in Bombay and expressed his total confidence in them.

Unlike the earlier ventures, the Anglo-Portuguese expedition against Kolaba was to be an overland attack supported by the combined fleets from the sea. The armies of the two nations were to assemble at the Portuguese port of Chaul and from there, march the 18 kilometres to Kolaba. The combined fleets would close in on Kolaba from the sea and bombard the place with their powerful guns.

Meanwhile, Angre heard about the Anglo-Portuguese build up and activated his network of spies in Bombay and Chaul. They unearthed the plan of an overland attack on Kolaba and Angre made preparations accordingly. He informed the Maratha King at Satara and the peshwa of the impending attack and the danger to the Konkan. The peshwa dispatched Pilaji Jadav with an advance guard of about 2,000 infantry and cavalry. The peshwa also sent word that if necessary he would personally come to Angre's help.

The Viceroy of Goa and the Portuguese of the North assembled their forces at Chaul, about 50 kilometres south of Bombay. The English contingent joined them there. From the start there were problems. The Portuguese regarded themselves superior to the English clerks and merchants who had been drafted for military service while the English looked upon the Portuguese with disdain. The General of the North and the Portuguese Viceroy took an instant dislike to the arrogant Commodore Matthews.

The Anglo-Portuguese contingent marched off to Kolaba. However, their heavier guns could not be taken across a river en route as neither ally had constructed a bridge across it and each thought that the other ally had built it. Finally, only the lighter cannons could accompany them. The navy meanwhile, closed in on Kolaba menacingly, but one of the English captains, anxious to bring his guns to bear on the fort ran his warship, the *Shoreham*, onto the rocks.

Commodore Matthews with his retinue, venturing out too far to reconnoitre the enemy's position, was attacked by one of Angre's troopers and received a lance wound in the thigh. Matthews, a man of notoriously violent temper, flew into a rage and 'galloping after the trooper, fired at him his two pistols, only to find that he had forgotten to load them.' On the other hand, the Viceroy of Goa complained of illness and retired to his cabin aboard the ship.

Angre, forewarned of the allied attack, had prepared well to face it. He had stocked the fort with ammunition for his powerful artillery. He had also assembled 1,000 infantry and 700 cavalry inside the fort and felt that more troops would clutter up the fort. He also stocked plenty of food, fodder and grain.

The English made a brave attempt to storm the fort and got as far as the main gate, despite constant firing from the ramparts of the fort. As they could not force open the gates, the more determined among them scaled the walls, but were cut down in hand-to-hand fighting, while those bunched up at the gate received the full fury of the

firing by the Indians. They were finally driven back to their camp with the loss of several of their guns and abandoned nearly all their ammunition. They also left behind over a hundred soldiers dead and wounded.

The Portuguese led by the General of the North, had also reached the fort walls. Kanhoji Angre ordered Pilaji Jadav's cavalry, which had been held back in reserve, to take on the Portuguese. The Marathas delight in wild cavalry charges, flashing their long-bladed *pattas* and razor-sharp lances. The Portuguese, without their heavier guns, which had been left at the unbridged river, could not stand the shock of the charge and they broke and fled.

Meanwhile, the fiery Commodore Matthews, who had been closely following the battle from his flagship, once again flew into a rage. Furious at the defeat, he was certain it was due to Portuguese treachery. He rushed to the Portuguese camp and hysterical with rage, he accused the General of the North, of treachery and cowardice and to enforce his argument, he shoved his baton into the mouth of the Portuguese General and was hardly less discourteous to the Viceroy of Goa. No further cooperation between the allies was possible after the Commodore's conduct.

Meanwhile, the redoubtable Maratha Peshwa himself appeared on the scene at the head of a powerful cavalry force. Whatever chances the Portuguese and the English felt they had, now vanished. Seeing the menacing presence of the peshwa's troops, they deemed it was far healthier to return home quickly. The Portuguese dashed back to Chaul and the English sailed back as fast as they could to Bombay.

After this fourth disaster, Boone finally gave up attempting to reduce Angre's strongholds. He laid down office and sailed back to England. According to British records, 'He was a governor of outstanding merit'.

The unmitigated disaster of the Anglo-Portuguese expedition undoubtedly contributed to Kanhoji Angre's prestige and the stout old Maratha Admiral sailed the Arabian Sea in triumph and remained a terror of the western cost.

# 11

# Chittorgarh

The great fortress of Chittorgarh is rooted deep in the psyche of the Rajputs and there is sanctity in the very name. It has figured so prominently in the history of Mewar that a brief description is absolutely necessary. I first saw Chittor as a little boy and the long narrow fortress built upon a flat-topped hill appeared like a great big battleship to me. I visited it several times in later years and studied it in some detail.

Located in south-east Rajasthan at a distance of about 90 kilometres from Udaipur, the fort stands on a flat-topped hill which rises 500 feet above the surrounding country and has precipitous cliffs on all sides; ideal for defence. The fort is almost 6 kilometres long north to south but less than a kilometre at its widest. The massive walls and battlements measuring 14 kilometres in length are so wide that 'a team of eight horses could gallop their summit'. These are pierced with numerous loopholes for the use of firearms. The steep serpentine approach to the fort is guarded by seven massive gateways, with lofty passages located at strategic points. Inside the fort are temples, palaces, bazaars, schools, water sources; home for an entire community. There are two monumental towers to commemorate great victories as well.

In the sixth century, the Maurya or Mori were a recognised power in the Chittor region. Bappa Rawal of Gehlot lineage (later known as Sisodia) came over from Saurashtra and captured the fortress around 883 AD. He established the capital and for six centuries after Bappa Rawal, the Gehlot banner, bearing the golden sun on a crimson field, flew proudly from the ramparts of Chittor. Battles were fought and victories won. *Khuman Rasa*, the ancient Mewar chronicle quoted by James Tod, records an Islamic invasion during the reign of Khuman. The invasion was led from Sindh by Mahmoon, a son of the famous Caliph Haroun-al-Rashid. The history of the Caliphs emphasises only successful expeditions and seldom alludes to those that failed. According to the *Khuman Rasa*, Khuman at the head of thirty-eight princes whose names are listed, representing the flower of Rajput chivalry, not only defended Chittor but led out his forces and routed the Arabs. Why else would the Arabs be restricted for ages, to the bleak and inhospitable desert sands of Sindh?

*Chittor Fort*

Allauddin Khilji

We shall leave the dust of centuries undisturbed, till we come to 1300 AD when Rawal Ratan Singh was on the throne at Chittor and Allauddin Khilji was the sultan at Delhi. For Allauddin it was important to secure the trade route that led to the prosperous ports of Gujarat.Rajasthan lay on the way and for the sultan's purpose the powerful forts of Rajasthan would have to be overrun. The siege of Jaisalmer lasted several years, but in 1301 Ranthambore was captured from the Rajputs. He then turned to Chittor.

According to several sources, there was another reason for Allauddin attacking Chittor. This was his desire for the beautiful Padmini, the wife of Ratan Singh, the ruler of Mewar. Malik Mohammad Jayasi in his text entitled *Padmavat* written around 1540, states that Princess Padmini was the daughter of Hamir Sank Chauhan of Sri Lanka. She was renowned for her beauty and peerless qualities. Hearing about her, Rawal Ratan Singh travelled to Sri Lanka to press his suit. He succeeded in winning her love and also her hand in marriage and brought her back to Chittor. The bards from Jaisalmer however claim that Padmini was a girl of the Bhatti clan, daughter of the exiled Rawal Punpal. Ratan Singh and Padmini had an idyllic existence together at Chittor. *Padmavat* however adds that her beauty was to be the cause of woes and their happiness was not fated to last.

Rani Padmavati

The fame of her dusky and lotus like beauty spread across the country. Sultan Allauddin, hearing about this at Delhi, determined to make her a part of his harem. Allauddin himself, according to a historian was 'an illiterate of unendearing presence and unremarkable physique as well as scruple free instincts.' Unprepossessing men, as if to compensate, yearn and lust for beautiful women.

Amir Khusrau, the court based writer-poet, accompanied the sultan on his excursion to Chittor. While he makes no direct mention of the Padmini episode, (indeed as a courtier he could not have) historians have pointed out that in his narrative there are several hints of it. Amir Khusrau compares Allauddin to King Solomon and writes about a queen as lovely as Sheba being in the fortress of Chittor.

All this has led some contemporary historians to suggest that the story of Padmini cannot be rejected as a figment of literary imagination. One can say that the invasion by Allauddin was prompted as much by the desire for conquest as by his infatuation for the peerless Padmini.

Allauddin with the forces of Delhi behind him attacked Chittor. But this great fort stood firm and repeated attempts by Allauddin were foiled by the brave defenders. Much has been documented about the siege and the valour of Rajputs. Prominent among these were Rana Lakshman Singh (or Lakumsi) of the Sisodia clan, Padmini's uncle Gorah and his nephew Badal.

After seven months of frustration, Allauddin decided on another tactic and sent a message to Ratan Singh begging that he be permitted one glimpse of Queen

*The beautiful palace of Rani Padmini*

Padmini, after which he would leave the region and return to his capital. This message, says Jayasi's *Padmavat*, led to much discussion within the fortress. This is hardly surprising, since the prevailing custom of *purdah* and veiling precluded outsiders from looking at high born women living in *rawalas* and *zenanas* (women's quarters). Here was a matter that completely breached etiquette, *Padmavat* tells that Allauddin was finally allowed to enter Chittor Fort and gaze not on Padmini but on her reflected image. He readily agreed to this and relying on the good faith of the Rajputs he entered the fort lightly guarded. The queen was asked to stand on the steps beside a small lake within the palace complex. She was kept out of the direct line of the sultan's vision,but he was permitted to view her reflected image in the lake through a strategically placed mirror. But the reflection itself was so bewitching that Allauddin's 'unendearing' face lit up. In a flash, Ratan Singh threw his goblet into the water and the ripples broke the spell which had obviously fallen over Allauddin.

The sultan was then courteously escorted back by Ratan Singh and to reciprocate the trust of the sultan, Ratan Singh accompanied him well beyond the gates of the fortress. But Ratan Singh had not reckoned with the perfidy of the Afghan and as per the latter's plan, Ratan Singh was treacherously ambushed and made prisoner.

A communication was sent that the Rawal would only be released, if Padmini was surrendered to the sultan. There was despair and consternation in Chittor. It was impossible for Rajputs to abandon either their king or Padmini. A clever scheme was devised by Padmini's uncle Gorah and his nephew Badal for the rescue of Ratan Singh without hazarding Padmini's life or honour. Intimation was dispatched to Allauddin that Padmini would be surrendered the day he withdrew his forces. He was also told that in keeping with her high status, she would be accompanied by her handmaidens and friends, some of whom would accompany her to Delhi. Allauddin was strictly warned against violating their privacy. He agreed to this. When it became clear that, as per the agreement Allauddin was breaking camp to withdraw his troops; the Rajputs started fulfilling their side of the bargain. A whole procession of 700 covered palanquins wound their way down to the enemy camp, watched with curiosity by Allauddin's departing troops. However, instead of Padmini's entourage, each palanquin carried the bravest defenders of Chittor borne by six fully armed soldiers disguised as litter bearers. But Allauddin had no suspicion of the ruse. The litters reached the enemy camp and were deposited within the *kanats* (walls of cloth). Half an hour was granted for a parting interview between Ratan Singh and his wife. The time was almost up, when instead of Padmini, the warriors emerged from the litters. There was utter confusion in Allauddin's camp and Ratan Singh mounting a fleet horse kept ready for him, made for the fortress. Gorah and Badal, leading the devoted band covered Ratan Singh's retreat and created havoc in the enemy ranks. They particularly targeted Allauddin but he was too well protected.

*Walls of Chittorgarh fort*

The choicest heroes of Chittor, motivated by the noble sentiments of freedom of their king and the honour of their queen, devoted themselves with ferocity to destruction. Few of them survived. Gorah was killed and Badal, a stripling of twelve, though wounded, escaped. Allauddin was defeated in his objective and the havoc they had made in his ranks, along with the dread of their continued resistance, forced him to give up his enterprise.

The *Khuman Rasa* describes a dialogue between Gorah's wife and young Badal, who though wounded, had escaped. She desires him to relate how her lord conducted himself in battle. The boy replies, 'He was the reaper of the harvest of battle: I followed his steps as the humble gleaner of his sword. On the gory bed of honour he spread a carpet of the slain; a barbarian prince his pillow, he laid him down and sleeps surrounded by the foe.' Again she says, 'Tell me, Badal how did my love behave?' Badal replies, 'Oh, mother! how further describe his deeds, when he left no foe to dread or admire him?' She smiles farewell and adds, 'My lord will chide my delay,' and springs into the flame.

Allauddin was obliged to retreat but some years later, having recouped his strength, returned to Chittor. On the other hand, Ratan Singh had not recovered from the loss of the valiant men who had sacrificed themselves. Allauddin came with overwhelming strength and carried on his attacks more closely, and when further resistance seemed impossible, the Rajputs preferred death to disgrace. James Tod describes the awful sacrifice which was to precede this act of devotion. This was the rite of *jauhar* where the women are immolated to preserve them from being polluted by the enemy's lust. Within the great subterranean retreat, which was impervious to the light of day, the funeral pyre was lighted and the soldiers of

Chittor beheld in procession the queens, their own wives and daughters numbering to several thousands. The lovely Padmini closed the throng and they entered the cavern where they could find security from dishonour in the devouring fire. The women hurling themselves into the fire and the men going out in a still brighter blaze of glory. This was fanaticism—Rajput fanaticism—how else could one describe it.

The Rana then called his devoted clans, for whom life no longer had any meaning. They threw open the gate and descended to the plains and with a reckless despair carried death or met it in the crowded ranks of the enemy. The sultan took possession of an inanimate capital, strewed with brave defenders, the smoke yet issuing from the cavern where lay the once fair object of his desire. A frustrated Allauddin committed every act of barbarity and vandalism in Chittor which his bigoted zeal could suggest, overthrowing temples and other monuments of art. He then handed the city to Maldeo, the Hindu chief of Jalore, who was one of his vassals.

*Place near which the annual Jauhar Mela took place*

After the fall of Chittor, the Sisodias, as the Gehlots clan now called themselves, withdrew to Kelwara where the magnificent fortress of Kumbhalgarh was later constructed. This was an almost inaccessible mountain retreat deep in the interior of the Aravallis. Here, they attempted to rebuild the tattered might of Mewar. In 1314, the valorous Hamir became the Rana. His main aim was to recapture Chittor and restore the prestige of Mewar. At Kelwara, 'Hamir unsheathed his sword which in future was never to remain far from his hand' and from there attacked the foe whenever opportunity offered. He desolated the plains and left only the fortified towns which the enemy could safely inhabit. The roads were rendered impassable by his men who often issued from their retreats in the Aravalli mountains and having done their work of devastation withdrew through the intricate ravines, baffling all pursuit. No cultivation or other peaceful activities were permitted by Hamir in the occupied territory. This 'scorched earth' policy and guerilla warfare had been used by the Rajput from the tenth century to the last of the Mughals in the eighteenth century.

Maldeo, the governor of Chittor, was helpless against such warfare. All trade, communication and other peaceful pursuit had to be abandoned. There are many romantic stories about Hamir and the way he recaptured Chittor. One version is that Maldeo finally tried to appease Hamir to put an end to his destructive policy, by sending him a proposal of marriage to a Chittor chieftain's daughter. Hamir married this girl and it was she along with a minister of Maldeo, who helped him in recapturing Chittor. She signalled Hamir at a time when Maldeo and his troops had gone on a military expedition. Hamir arrived in force and dealt with Maldeo's reserve troops. He was soon the master of the fortress, which he described as being 'moistened by the blood of my ancestors'. Thus once again 'the standard of the sun' shone resplendent from the walls of Chittor. Maldeo not being strong enough to mount an assault carried the news to Sultan Mohammad-bin-Tughlak who now ruled at Delhi. The adherents of Hamir returned to their ancient abode and the highlands poured forth their men and the Mewaris rejoiced once more, throwing off the foreign yoke.

Some traditions also state that Sultan Mohammad-bin-Tughlak himself or one of his generals advanced to recover Chittor. Unwisely however he marched by the eastern plateau where the difficult terrain is a major hazard and rendered his superior numbers useless. Hamir, assisted by all the chiefs of Mewar engaged the Tughlak army at Singoli and routed the enemy, capturing vast tracts of territory including Ajmer and Ranthambore. Hamir's name became synonymous with gallantry and valour. For the next two centuries Mewar enjoyed power and property greater than any other period of its history.

It is stated that an inscription in a Jain temple dated 1438 AD, records this victory of Hamir's over the forces at Delhi. The recovery of large tracts of territory and Mewar's wonted splendour also provide confirmation. Contemporary chronicles note that all Tughlak sultans left Rajasthan severely alone.

We now move forward to the early 1500s when Rana Sanga, who is referred to as the *kallas* (crown) of Mewar was ruling. Sanga had won eighteen pitched battles against the kings of Delhi and Malwa. He carried eighty wounds on his body from swords and lances. Alarmed by his designs, the Sultans of Malwa and Gujarat combined their armies against Sanga, but were not only routed in battle but Muzaffar, the Sultan of Malwa was also captured. This defeat festered in the minds of the two sultans and several years later, after Sanga's death in 1528, Bahadur Shah, the Sultan of Gujarat and his ally, the Sultan of Malwa decided to avenge the earlier defeat and insult. At this time, Bikramjeet was the Rana at Chittor, a young and arrogant man who was totally oblivious of the external dangers which threatened his kingdom. He was also utterly regardless of the respect which his proud nobles expected. He is said to have enjoyed deliberately insulting old courtiers and noblemen, as a result of which many loyal kinsmen left the capital and returned to their *jagir* lands. Bikramjeet's misrule thus led to open rupture bordering on rebellion.

Another reason for discord between the Rana and his nobles was their total disagreement on the organisation of the army and military tactics. The Rajputs had belatedly realised the importance of artillery and while the Rana favoured the *paek*

*The burning of the Rajput women during the siege of Chittor*

(foot soldiers) for the protection of the artillery, the Rajput nobles despised the infantry and preferred the glory of the mounted cavalry warrior.

Bahadur Shah of Gujarat felt he should take advantage of the dissensions in Mewar. He had the support of the Malwa troops and also brought along European artillery experts and an engineer named Labri Khan of Ferghana. This was thus a very powerful effort against Mewar.

Since the vassals of Mewar were estranged from Rana Bikramjeet, it was Queen Mother Karnavati who made a stirring call to arms for the defence of the ancestral fort of Chittor. The very name of Chittor conjures magic in the heart of the Rajput and the Queen Mother's appeal rallied the alienated nobles and ordinary soldiers alike under the Sisodia banner. Many of the disgruntled vassals who had left the capital because of the ill-treatment shown by the Rana responded to the Queen's fervent appeal. She also sent the unpopular Rana Bikramjeet away to Bundi.

Despite the odds and the belated preparation, the warriors of Mewar put up a valiant resistance. Eventually the artillery of the sultans proved decisive. A mine placed at the 'Beeka rock' blew up a large part of the rampart where the Haras had been posted. Rao Durga moved in swiftly with his men to defend the breach and many assaults were repelled. Even Queen Jawahir Bai, clad in armour headed a sally in which she was slain.

In the face of the hopeless situation, Chittor once again took the decision in March 1535 for the awesome finality of the *jauhar* and the accompanying *saka* for yet another time in its history. It was the firm belief of the Sisodias that the ancient fort can be defended only by royalty. Rana Bikramjeet was not present in Chittor, having been sent away by the Queen Mother. The Rajputs then took recourse to the expedient of crowning a king as a sacrifice, so that the dignity of the guardian goddess of Chittor is protected. Baghji, the prince of Deolia, courted the insignia of destruction; the banner of Mewar floated over him, and the golden sun on its crimson field shone brightly when the *changi* (royal canopy) was raised over his head amidst the shouts of her defenders. Thus, as required, the warriors of Chittor were once again led by a king.

The decision for the *jauhar* and the *saka* having been already taken, Queen Karnavati and the other women went through the rituals and prepared for immolation; they entered the chamber full of explosives and gunpowder and soon their lives were extinguished. The men having nothing left to live for, donned their *kesariya* (saffron robes), mounted their horses, threw open the gates, unsheathed their swords and lances and led by the newly crowned Baghji of Deolia, charged out to fight till the last man.

The fort came into the hands of Sultan Bahadur Shah of Gujarat but he could not retain it for more than a fortnight. Some historians maintain that as soon as Bahadur Shah left Chittor, the Rajputs reoccupied it. Another version is that Mughal troops arrived at Chittor and Bahadur was forced to withdraw from there. Yet a third story, which has become part of folklore is that Queen Karnavati had sent a *rakhi* by a messenger to the Mughal King Humayun, which made him her 'bracelet brother' and bound him to defend her cause. During the siege, Karnavati had sent word to Humayun that as her *rakhi* brother, he had to fulfill his pledge and succour Chittor. He proved himself a true brother and abandoned his conquests in Bengal and came to Chittor, although belatedly. He expelled Bahadur Shah from the fortress and also took Mandu, the capital of Malwa, by assault, as punishment for the chief who had sided with the Sultan of Gujarat. Humayun reinstated Bikramjeet by girding him with a sword. However many historians find no evidence to support this version as Humayun did not visit Chittor till a couple of years later.

With the Rajputs once again in possession of Chittor, Rana Bikramjeet returned to reoccupy the throne. He had however learnt nothing from adversity and continued his insolent behaviour. But that is a different story and does not belong here.

Barely thirty-two years later, Chittor had to go through the agony of the *jauhar* and the accompanying *saka* for the third and last time. In 1567, the Mughal Emperor Akbar turned to Mewar as part of his policy of territorial expansion. In the first assault by Allauddin Khilji, twelve crowned heads had defended the crimson banner of Mewar to death. In the second sack of Chittor, Baghji of Deolia, a noble scion of Mewar, claimed the crown of martyrdom. But on this, the third and grandest struggle, there was no royal to defend the sacred fort and the mysterious tie which bound the race of Gehlots with the guardian goddess of Chittor was broken. Rana Udai Singh, dishonouring the Rajput tradition, fled from the battlefield. This thousand-year-old abode of royalty then became the refuge of wild beasts and Chittor, the sanctified capital lay desecrated.

Akbar focussed on Mewar to augment his hold on Rajasthan. The warrior spirit of the Rajputs and the harsh deserts had discouraged successive foreign invaders from overrunning Rajasthan. Akbar also felt that the friendship or defeat of Mewar would have a major impact on potential rivals and also secure the traditional trade and campaign routes from Delhi to the seaports of Gujarat.

Rana Udai Singh behaved in a manner quite different from the traditional image of the Rajput who through history had preferred death to dishonor. He left Chittor to be defended by 8,000 Rajputs under the command of an experienced and trusted commander, Jaimal, the Rathore chief of Badnor. For this action Udai Singh has been vilified as 'a craven prince and a coward'. But others feel it was a tactical withdrawal, for he had provisioned Chittor well and laid waste the surrounding countryside to prevent the Mughals from gathering local food. It was not certain that Chittor would fall and even if it did, the Mughals would be capturing nothing more than a strong outpost of Mewar's vast territory.

The Chittor garrison had warriors like Sahidas of Salumber, Rawat Duda who led the sons of Sanga and other noble chiefs, some descended from Prithviraj of Delhi. But the names that shine brightest in this gloomy page of the story of Mewar were Jaimal of Badnor and the sixteen-year-old Patta.

Akbar arrived below the fort of Chittor in great strength. It is recorded that his camp extended 16 kilometres. Although some chroniclers make this out to be a holy war against infidels, Akbar's army had Hindu commanders like Todar Mal, Bhagwan Das and others. The siege lasted almost a year and was personally led by Akbar, who was then a young man of twenty-five years of age.

*Akbar shoots Jaimal at the siege of Chittor*

The Mughals erected batteries of canons for bombarding inside the fort, but this was not very effective because the guns had to fire at steeply vertical angles and as the high targets were not visible, accuracy was poor. He then resorted to laying mines to breach the walls. The soldiers had to burrow under the rock until they reached a position beneath the walls, where they would excavate a chamber and pack it with gunpowder which would then be exploded to breach the walls. But the defenders could see them at work and they were therefore easy targets. As a result, casualties among the Mughal troops were high in the mining process. The emperor then resorted to a device known as the *sabat* (covered way). This involved building a structure consisting of side walls of rubble and mud, which could resist cannon balls and a thick wooden roof held together with hides. This covered way was huge and 'wide enough for ten horsemen to ride abreast and high enough for a man on an elephant to pass along'. The *sabat* grew steadily in length towards the fort walls. In the side walls of the *sabat,* there were chambers with loopholes like any fort to house cannons and musketeers. According to Abul Fazl, the *sabat* followed a zig-zag course so that the fort walls ahead would be visible and easy to target for the Mughal cannons hidden inside. The front end of the covered way snaking towards the fort was under constant construction. It was thus a very dangerous place to work because the Rajputs kept firing cannon balls and musket shots at the front construction area. The workers were protected by movable screens but as the *sabat* advanced slowly but steadily nearer and nearer the walls of the fort, the advantage shifted towards the attackers. The cannons concealed in the *sabat* advanced close and they could do far greater damage, both because of greater impact of the shot and better targeting. As the large mouth of the *sabat* reached the walls, the men could force a hole in the fort.

At long last, the Mughal forces managed to make a crack in the walls which was fiercely defended by the Rajputs. Sahidas of Salumber fell fighting at 'the gate of the sun' and his altar still stands at the spot. Many clan chieftains also died fighting.

Jaimal of Badnor and young Patta of Kailwa, all of sixteen years of age, played a major role in the action. Jaimal had climbed the rampart to inspect the ongoing repair when a lone marksman picked him out. The matchlock it is claimed was fired by Akbar himself. Jaimal's leg was shattered but he was not killed. With their commander disabled and the northern defences destroyed, they saw no hope of salvation. The fatal *jauhar* was then commanded. To the chanting of verses from the scriptures, women dressed in bridal finery led the children, the old and the servants to the *mahasati*. While the fire consumed them, 8,000 Rajputs ate the last *beera* (betel leaf given to departing guests) together and put on their saffron robes and the gates were thrown open. Jaimal, though on the brink of death, insisted on being hoisted up on the horse and held up there by a companion. Young Patta was by his side and they led the charge down the steep slope. Behind them were the mounted clans, dressed in saffron, a spring of the sacred *tulsi* (basil) held between clenched teeth. Accompanying them, with lances in their hands were Patta's mother and young wife. Not one survived to stain the tradition of inglorious surrender.

When Akbar entered Chittor, it was a dead city. His subsequent actions were totally uncharacteristic. He defaced all temples and palaces and ravaged the works of art. He removed from the city all symbols of regality; the grand battle drums, treasure and even the carved portals which were taken to Akbar's fort in Agra. He went further and ordered the massacre of 30,000 peasants who had sought refuge in the fort. This was the only example of carnage ordered by Akbar and has remained an unredeemed blot on an otherwise illustrious career.

He however showed more sensitivity when he recognised the merits of his foes and ordered the construction of two memorials at Agra commemorating the valour of Jaimal and Patta.

This was the third and last sack of Chittor.

12

# Rana Kumbha of Mewar

Rana Kumbha was one of the most gifted kings in the history of this country. According to traditional Hindu records, an ideal king would combine the qualities of a *chakravartin* (universal ruler) warrior, who would strive to provide protection to all his subjects along with possessing a high scholastic and intellectual stature. The ideal ruler was further expected to provide patronage to artists and intellectuals, donate liberally to charities and religious centres, and also encourage the construction of temples and works of public utility, trade and commerce. This was indeed, a lot to expect from an individual and few did live up to this standard. Rana Kumbha was one of those few.

The thirty-six warrior clans of Rajasthan claim descent from the sun, moon and fire. A more modern interpretation would hold that mythology conceals a more rational truth, namely that the first ancestor was as powerful as the sun or fire or as serene and luminous as the moon. The first among these clans are the princes of Mewar. Mewar was the only dynasty, with the exception of Jaisalmer, which held onto its sovereignty and territory for eight centuries since the first invaders from Central Asia crossed the Indus.

Rana Kumbha came to the throne at a very young age in 1433 when his father Rana Mokal was assassinated. Thus Kumbha succeeded in an uncertain atmosphere of conspiracies, intrigues and confusion. One group of nobles took up the claim of Mokal's murderer, declaring him the king of a part of Mewar. Meanwhile, various chiefs of areas lying on the borders of Mewar also made bids for independence from the central authority. In addition to these internal problems, there existed a very real danger from the neighbouring Muslim kingdoms of Malwa and Gujarat.

As Kumbha was just a boy, his mother felt threatened by the various factions at court and asked her father Ranmal, who was a Rathore prince of Jodhpur to come down to Chittor and help protect her son. Ranmal came with his Rathore troops and did indeed help in restoring law and order and was of considerable help to young Kumbha. Ranmal soon established himself in Mewar but being a Rajput whose creed is to acquire land or better still a kingdom, his presence in Mewar became a danger of its own. He was from the arid desert regions of Marwar and coveted the fertile fields of Mewar. Such are the twists and turns of fate that Ranmal, who came as a protector, soon became a predator. It became apparent to the Queen mother that her own family's motives were distinctly suspicious and they were out to defraud her own child. Thoroughly alarmed, she remonstrated with her father, but the only reply was a hint threatening the life of her child.

It is not necessary to go into the details but this major danger posed by the ambitious and covetous Ranmal was dealt with by the Sisodia clan of Mewar, who were deeply loyal to their boy king Kumbha. There was already distrust and quarrels between the local Sisodia and the Rathore nobles from Marwar and their men-at-arms. Peaceful coexistence between the two equally battle-hardy and proud clans became impossible within the confines of a single fortress. The Sisodias unsheathed their swords one night and in well-planned clandestine action they fell on

the Rathore troops and cut them to pieces. The end of Ranmal, well worth recounting, was more ludicrous than tragic. The old chief intoxicated with love, wine and opium had a young handmaiden in his embrace and heard nothing of the tumult. The young girl, rising gently, dexterously bound the unwelcome and drunken lover to his bed with his own turban. Before the dazed man realised what was happening, the soldiers had entered. Wild with rage, he tried to extricate himself and by some virtuosity of movement, he got upon his legs, his bed still tied to his back like a shell. With no weapons except a brass vessel he levelled to the ground more than one assailant before a shot from a matchlock killed him.

Peace returned to Mewar, some years passed and Kumbha grew up. He first secured his position internally and consolidated his rule within the realm. Then he turned to his neighbours. He carried his arms to Sirohi in the west so as to strengthen his position against the Sultan of Gujarat. He seized the mountainous area of Abu and Ranakpur from the kingdom of Sirohi. Then he turned north and took over Sambhar and Amber, thus securing his border against the Muslim king of Malwa. Kumbha then moved towards his erstwhile enemies of Marwar, whose capital Mandore had already been infested by Kumbha's army. Kumbha next attacked the Khan of Nagaur in the north and wrested from him Nagaur, Ajmer and Chatsu. In the south, he also secured the Zawar area from the kingdom of Dungarpur. Didwana and Ranthambore were also annexed. Didwana was an important town for its salt industry. The tracts of Malpura, Narwar and Bundi were captured too and retained or returned back to their rulers in exchange for acknowledging Kumbha's sovereignty. The Ranakpur inscription of 1439 bears witness and details all these conquests of Kumbha.

Kumbha's vigorous strategy led to a remarkable expansion of the boundaries of Mewar in addition to which he acquired huge wealth from ransoms, indemnities and pure loot. This helped him finance his later wars and the civil development of the kingdom as well as arts and architecture.

The world over, traditional chroniclers and bards extol and glorify those kings who grandly conquer neighbouring or distant lands. Most of the inscriptions available to historians today celebrate victorious, all-conquering kings. There are other kings and chiefs who worked more toward ensuring peace and justice for their subjects. The latter categories were only mildly lauded. They do not provide for soul-stirring poetry or prose. Kumbha's later concentration on art and architecture and the works of public utility and encouragement of trade and commerce, which we deal with later, have received somewhat less attention. But we have to revert first to his warlike and glorious feats on the battlefield.

There was a long standing rivalry between Mewar and Malwa. This was inevitable as they had a long common frontier, apart from which exiled nobles from one kingdom often sought and got shelter and status at the rival court. Even Kumbha's heroic stepbrother Chonda had, at one stage, been forced to seek shelter at Mandu, the capital of Malwa, but that is a different story.

In the year 1436, the throne of Malwa was usurped by one of the court nobles Mahmud Khalji. The son of the King of Malwa visited Kumbha and appealed for his help against Mahmud. Kumbha advanced into Malwa and burned down the stronghold of Sarangpur and inflicted much damage on the Malwa territory. The hostilities escalated and the armies of Mewar and Malwa clashed at Sarangpur in 1437. The Malwa army was ignominiously routed. According to bardic tradition which is repeated in the Ranpur and Kumbhalgarh inscriptions, after the sack of Sarangpur, Kumbha took countless enemy soldiers prisoner. Rana Kumbha then laid siege to Mandu, the beautiful capital of Malwa situated in the forested mountains, and carried off its new Sultan Mahmud Khalji and kept him captive at Chittor for six months. Abul Fazl, the sixteenth-century Mughal historian, records this victory and praises Kumbha's greatness of soul in setting his enemy free not only without ransom but with gifts.

However, five years later in 1442 Mahmud Khalji marched against Mewar to avenge his earlier defeat. He first assaulted the fort of Kumbhalgarh and even Chittor but failed to make any impression. Ahmad Shah, the Sultan of Gujarat also tried to make trouble for Kumbha at the same time on the western border but had to retire with heavy losses.

The two Muslim kings of Gujarat and Malwa realised that individually they had had no success. Thus several years later, in 1457 the two decided to combine their forces and jointly attack Mewar. Kumbha now had a two-front war on his hands. The Sultan of Gujarat first attacked Kumbhalgarh, while the King of Malwa directed his efforts against Mandalgarh. The well-known historian Ferishta has recorded this war and is backed up by the Kumbhalgarh inscription. Rana Kumbha met the combined forces on the plains of Malwa bordering his own state. At the head of 1,00,000 horses and foot soldiers and 1,400 elephants, Kumbha inflicted a crushing defeat on the two sultans. Even though mentioned in the chronicles, I believe that these figures are probably exaggerated.

To commemorate this victory, Kumbha erected the famous landmark of Chittor, the Vijay Stambh (Tower of Victory). It has nine storeys and rises to a height of 37 metres. The architect for the tower was Jaita assisted by his sons and it took eight years to complete this 'ringlet on the brow of Chittor'. It is decorated with sculpture and friezes both inside and on the external surfaces, while an internal staircase runs through the whole. The only surviving tablet records the following, 'Shaking the earth, the lords of Gujjar Khand and Malwa, both the Sultans with armies overwhelming as the ocean, invaded Medpat. Koombhkarna (another name for Kumbha) reflected lustre on the land to what point can we exalt his renoun? In the midst of the armies

*Vijay Stambh at Chittor*

of the foe, Kumbha was as a tiger or as a flame in a dry forest. While the sun continues to warm the earth, so long may the fame of Rana Kumbha endure…'

The victories of Kumbha are detailed in various contemporary sources, such as inscriptions, copper plates and several Persian texts which belong in history books and it is unnecessary to quote them here. An important development of these victories was that they provided natural frontiers to the state. These were guarded by a clan of well garrisoned fortresses, particularly the mountain passes. There were a total of eighty-four fortresses for the defence of Mewar and out of these, thirty-two were built by Kumbha. Second only to Chittor is the picturesque and impregnable fort of Kumbhalgarh, which was also used by the Rana as a second capital. Kumbhalgarh is important not only as a military fortification but also for the architectural gems it contains inside. But before we talk about Kumbhalgarh we must focus attention on Kumbha's remarkable architect Mandan.

The eminent historian Rima Hooja writes, 'To some extent, we may say that the architecture of Kumbha's reign is inseparable from both, the flamboyant Maharana himself and his *sutradhar* (architect/artisan) Mandan, son of Kshetra, whose texts were

*Kumbhalgarh Fort: Designed by Mandan, it was considered impregnable*

useful to contemporary and later architects. In an age of numerous architects and effusive building activity, Mandan holds a special space because alongside working as an active architect, he compiled several Sanskrit manuscripts on architecture. These are the *Vastu Mandan*, *Rupa Mandan, Prasad Mandan*, *Raj Vallabh Mandan* and several more. Mandan personally gave substance to the instructions embodied in his texts by translating them into reality at the several building works put into his care by his discerning sovereign. Prominent amongst these is the fort of Kumbhalgarh.'

I have had the good fortune of visiting Kumbhalgarh on more than one occasion. The fort is located on a lofty hill rising steeply to a height of 3,500 feet. Battlements and bastions rise tier upon tier and the seven fortified gates positioned on the winding approach to the upper reaches ensured additional security for the main habitation area of the fort. The main battlement wall is broad enough for several horsemen to ride abreast across it. The area enclosed within the walls is huge; embracing several square kilometres and has beautiful temples, stables, armoury, storehouses etc. The summit of the hill, which lies within the fort, is crowned by the Badal Mahal (Palace of Clouds). It is a small structure that is built in marble and during the rains it appears to be floating in the clouds.

I was most intrigued by a novel architectural feature of Kumbhalgarh. The outer base walls are rounded or semi-spherical at close intervals. This type of construction is rarely seen in forts and after many enquiries from various sources I got some explanation. The rounded semi-spherical feature on the base walls was an important development in military architecture and is basically designed to deflect and resist cannonballs, which then ricochet. This feature must have been added at a later stage when cannons were in use.

Other than the several fortifications, Kumbha built new palaces across Mewar. The palace at Chittor named after Kumbha is now mostly in ruins, but it gives an idea of mid-fifteenth century pre-Mughal Rajput civil architecture. It was divided into two parts. The women's quarters were known as the *zenana* or *rawala* and the men's quarters were called the *mardana*. The women's quarters contained carved stone lattices through which the women could view the outside world or events taking place in the courtyards. The men's quarters contained large halls for public audience and the private apartments. The men's quarters also had a *sileh khana* (armoury), *daulat khana* (treasury) and several other rooms, including temples. The men's side was grander than the women's quarters.

Kumbha was not just a king who lived his life in the saddle and the battlefield. His reign was marked by good governance and prosperity for his subjects. Trade and commerce flourished and there was much travel between Mewar and other parts of South Asia. He also constructed water reservoirs, step wells and tanks. Many public inns, monasteries and schools were established throughout Mewar. He built a citadel Achalgarh at the peak of Abu and often used to reside in the cold climes.

Among the several temples that he constructed, one requires special mention—the one at Sadri Pass, which is a huge three-storeyed structure. The interior is inlaid with mosaics of cornelian, agate and other semi precious stones. Kumbha was a Hindu but the temple is dedicated to Jain saints.

Kumbha's accomplishments never seem to end. Not only was he a deeply learned man but also a poet of distinction. The Kumbhalgarh inscription states that writing poetry was as easy for him as going into battle. He was the author of four plays, some in Sanskrit, and an important work was the *Rasik-Priya* which is a commentary on the *Geet Govinda* (Divine Melodies). Apart from Sanskrit, Kumbha had mastery over several other Indian languages.

It is incredible but Kumbha was also an accomplished musician and played the *veena*. He had to his credit five texts on music and musical theory, among them the famous *Sangeet-Raja*. He had also composed several poetic invocations to various deities,

*Meera Bai:*
*One of the most mystical figures of Rajput history*

which he set to classical ragas and talas. Kumbha single-handedly ushered in a period of renaissance by encouraging art, architecture, music and learning.

Kumbha married the daughter of the Rathore of Mairta, the first of the clans of Marwar. Meera Bai was the most celebrated princess of her time for her beauty and romantic piety. Some of her odes and hymns to Krishna are still admired. Whether she imbibed her poetic piety from her husband, or whether from her he caught the sympathy which produced the sequel to the songs of Govinda, we cannot determine. Her history is a romance and her excessive devotion to her favourite deity, gave rise to many tales of scandal.

There is however another historical version that Meera was the wife of Prince Bhojraj, a son of Rana Sanga of Mewar and was widowed at a young age. Her father Ratan Singh, a prince of Jodhpur, was killed early in life on the battlefield. Meera turned to Krishna worship at a young age and it is her absolute devotion to Krishna and the bhakti poetry she composed that caused her to be revered as a saint.

*Rana Sanga riding a prized stallion*

Later, Meera Bai's devotion to Krishna increased and her family looked askance at her public singing and dancing before the idol of Krishna and keeping company with wandering holy men. Some years later, she left Chittor and went to Mairta, her parent's home but moved on to Vrindavan and Dwarka (possibly because her behaviour was too unconventional to be acceptable). There were also attempts on her life by members of her family. Meera's songs declare that the cup of poison sent to her and the snake in a basket were rendered harmless with the help of Krishna. She was asked to come back to Chittor but that night, she disappeared from the temple.

Kumbha mixed gallantry with his warlike pursuits. He carried off the daughter of the chief of Jhalawar who had been betrothed to the prince of Mundore; this renewed the old feud and the Rathore made many attempts to redeem his affianced bride, but in vain. On one occasion he almost succeeded in a surprise by escalade—having cut his way in the night through the forest in the least guarded part of the fort; but as the bard remarks: 'Though he cut his way through the *jhal* (brushwood), he could not reach the *Jhalani* (from Jhalawar).'

Kumbha had occupied the throne for half a century; he had triumphed over the enemies of his race, fortified his country with strongholds and embellished it with temples. The year which should have been a jubilee was disgraced by the foulest blot in the annals, and his life, which nature was about to close, terminated by the poignard of an assassin—his own son!

In 1469, Udai committed patricide. Such was the detestation against him that his name is left blank in the annals. Shunned by his kin, he tried to win allies by bestowing Sambhar and Ajmer districts on Jodhpur. He even humbled himself before the King of Delhi by offering his daughter in marriage, 'but heaven manifested its vengeance' and scarcely had he left the king 'when a flash of lighting struck the *hatiaro* (murderer) to the earth, whence he never arose.'

# 13

# Rani of Jhansi

The Rani of Jhansi is probably the most remarkable woman in Indian history. She was on scene for a brief period of five years but emerged as the most outstanding and charismatic leader of the great Revolt of 1857-59. Even her enemies rated her as 'the best and bravest of the rebel leaders.' In her short but luminous career, she did more than many rulers could aspire to do in several lifetimes. She fought British injustice and tyranny in battle after battle. She ruled Jhansi for the benefit of her people, and won not just their loyalty but their hearts. The rani made heroes out of the common people of Jhansi.

Strangely, there is not much literature about her and she lives more in the ballads, folktales and stories of Bundelkhand than in written accounts. She has often been compared to Joan of Arc, though the latter has inspired 12,000 volumes in French alone.

Jhansi was a medium-sized state and in the early 1850s, it is estimated to have covered an area of approximately 5,000 square kilometres. The state was part of an area known as Bundelkhand. Jhansi was part of the Maratha Confederacy, which was headed by the peshwa and included powerful kingdoms. In 1804, the ruler of Jhansi seeing the ascendant star of the British detached Jhansi from the crumbling Maratha Confederacy and signed a treaty with the British in which a crucial clause was that 'the British guaranteed the state to the ruler and his heirs in perpetuity.'

The rani's ancestors were Karhada Brahmins and came from the small town of Wye near Satara in Maharashtra. Lakshmi Bai's father, Moropant Tambe, was close confidant and advisor to the peshwa's brother Chimaji Appa.

When Peshwa Baji Rao II was defeated by the British in 1818, he had to leave Pune and live in exile at Bithur, a small town near Kanpur. His brother, Chimaji Appa, was also exiled but chose to live in Varanasi. Lakshmi Bai's father went with Chimaji to Varanasi, on a modest salary of fifty rupees a month.

Chimaji Appa lived in royal style and built himself a palace on the banks of the Ganga. Moropant and his wife Bhagirathi lived in a wing of this palace. They had a happy married life, and one child, a daughter whom they called Manakarnika. This is one of the names given to the holy river Ganga, in whose lap she was born in 1828. Manakarnika was called Manu till the time of her marriage. Lakshmi Bai was the name given to her by her husband's family and it was how she was known after she became the maharani.

Moropant's wife, Bhagirathi, was remarkably beautiful and she passed on her good looks to her daughter. Manu was happy in her early childhood, playing on the banks of the Ganga. But the stories of her childhood suggest that while she was a lively and high-spirited little girl, she was also very stubborn and difficult to control.

Chimaji Appa died in 1832 and the Tambe family had to move to Bithur. Here, Moropant joined the exiled court of the ex-Peshwa, Baji Rao II. Soon after having moved to Bithur, however, Bhagirathi also died and the task of bringing up Manu fell upon her father.

At Bithur, Manu came in contact with the peshwa's son, Nana Saheb, as well as Nana's nephew, Rao Saheb and Tatya Tope. These three, like herself, were destined to play major roles in the Revolt of 1857. Manu spent much of her time with Nana, Rao and Tatya. In their company she became quite a tomboy. She followed their example and learned to ride, shoot and wield the sword. She, in fact, became an excellent rider and an expert swordswoman, abilities which stood her in good stead in the later training of her troops and in her personal encounters with the enemy. She was also keen on physical exercise and ran races, flew kites and was better than most boys in all these activities.

On their cross-country rides, Manu used to tag along with Nana, Rao and Tatya. The story goes that on one such occasion, as two of the boys and Manu were galloping across the country, Nana, in trying to avoid a low branch of a tree, fell off his horse. He had a big gash on his head and lost much blood. On their return, much fuss was made about Nana's injury and he was made to rest. Manu found all this very amusing and said to him, 'Your forefathers were great warriors and look at you being coddled like this for a small cut in the head.'

Nana, peeved and nursing a headache, said, 'Manu, you are a nuisance and you talk too much. Now away with you.'

The next day, Nana chose to ride on an elephant and Manu again had a dig at him saying, 'Nana perhaps finds horse-riding a bit too tough and so has chosen an easy seat on the elephant.'

Nana, now thoroughly irritated, refused to let her accompany him on the howdah of the elephant. This enraged Manu, who got on her horse and riding close to Nana's elephant, shouted at him, 'You wait and see! For your one elephant, I will have ten. Mark my words!'

An advantage that Manu got from her association with the three boys was that she got an education. She used to sit with them for their lessons and so she learned to read and write. Manu became a forceful and determined person. Thus endowed with beauty, intellect and character, she had all the makings of a charismatic leader.

Vishnu Godse, a priest who lived in Jhansi at the time, has given a description of Manu in her early teens. He says that she was tall and slim, with a swan-like neck. Light of complexion, she had an oval face, a fine nose and large expressive eyes, as beautiful as the lotus. She was bright and full of chatter, and people took to her immediately.

When Manu was about twelve years old, it was time for her father to find a suitable match for her. The suitor had to be a Brahmin belonging to the Karhada sect. Suitors there were aplenty, horoscopes were compared, but no one could be identified. Time passed and Moropant's friends urged him not to delay any further as the girl had reached puberty. Soon a year was gone and still there was no prospect. Then came a proposal from the Maharaja of Jhansi, Gangadhar Rao.

Gangadhar Rao was a middle-aged man but he was able and scholarly and did much to pull the state of Jhansi out of the morass into which his previous two predecessors had left it. One of his notable achievements was that he built an excellent library of rare books. Theatre was another great interest and he was a patron. The neighbouring Bundela rulers of Panna, Orchha and Datia respected him and called him Kaka Saheb or uncle.

After Gangadhar lost his first wife, he did not marry for several years, even though the couple had remained childless. However, in 1852,Gangadhar decided that it was time to look for a suitable bride. Not having an heir was a constant source of worry not only for him, but also for the people of Jhansi, as this gave the British a chance to interfere in the succession.

The ex-Peshwa at Bithur was consulted for a suitable girl and he promptly suggested Manu. Gangadhar's emissary was very impressed by the lovely young girl, bright of eye and lithe of limb. Gangadhar readily agreed and when word reached Bithur, there was much celebration. Manu was going to be a maharani.

In May 1842, the maharaja and Manu were married at Jhansi. As was the custom, her name was changed by the family to Lakshmi Bai. The wedding was celebrated with much splendour. The couple walked round the fire seven times, and the priest tied one end of Lakshmi Bai's sari to the maharaja's sash. As he did so, Lakshmi Bai said clearly and audibly, 'Panditji, make the knot very firm.' A bride was supposed to be modest and shy, but Lakshmi Bai was neither. All the guests were startled and gasped but Gangadhar was touched.

Gangadhar was an orthodox Hindu and Lakshmi Bai soon found that as a maharani, she must remain in purdah. She was only fourteen or fifteen years old and after the comparative freedom at Bithur, she found the seclusion of purdah most irksome.

The Khas Mahal (main palace) was situated inside the fort and surrounded by a garden, The parade ground was a great boon for Lakshmi Bai. Since she was not allowed outside the fort, she used it for riding, physical exercise and other activities. Lakshmi Bai also started what was later to develop into a regiment for women. She started training her companions and maid servants in horsemanship and drill.

Since she was not interested in dance and theatre, Gangadhar asked her, 'Would you like to get acquainted with matters of government and the state?'

'There is nothing I would like more, maharaja,' replied a delighted Lakshmi Bai.

Soon, meeting and discussions with the *diwan* (chief minister) and other senior officials in the army and administration became a feature of her life. She was worried about the British presence in Jhansi. Under the treaty with them, an assistant political officer had been posted at Jhansi, as well as *sipahis* under British officers.

*Nana Saheb with his escort to meet rebel forces advancing from Malwa*

As time passed, Gangadhar became fond of the unusual and striking woman who was his wife. In 1851, he took her on a pilgrimage to her birthplace, Varanasi, as well as Gaya, Prayag and other places of religious interest. When they returned to Jhansi, there were reports that Lakshmi Bai was expecting a child. It had been seven years since they had been married, and there was great rejoicing when a son was born. Gangadhar, a bit infirm by now, was especially delighted with his infant son. Lord Dalhousie, the governor-general, would not be able to get his talons on Jhansi. But the rejoicing did not last long. When the heir was only three months old, he died. The couple was disconsolate, as were the people of Jhansi.

Soon after, Gangadhar's health started deteriorating. He was haunted by the prospect of his state being annexed by the British. Lord Dalhousie's main objective seemed to be to absorb the Indian states into British territory. He had already grabbed a few states where the rulers had died without natural heirs. Gangadhar knew that should he die without an heir, Jhansi state would lapse, but should he seek to adopt, the case might be decided by the government in his favour.

When Gangadhar finally realised that he was seriously ill, he adopted a child from another branch of the family. The boy, Anand Rao, was five years old and had descended from Gangadhar's grandfather.

The adoption ceremonies were conducted at Gangadhar's bedside, in the presence of the nobles of the court and two British representatives, Major Ellis, the assistant political agent and his colleague, so that they might officially witness the adoption. The child was given a new name, Damodar Rao. Gangadhar also wrote to Dalhousie referring to the treaty of 1817, which guaranteed the throne to the maharaja and 'his heirs and successors'. But as we see later the governor-general had other ideas. Two days later, on 21 November 1853, Gangadhar Rao breathed his last.

Lakshmi Bai became a widow at the age of twenty-five. After the maharaja's death, she was at a decisive turning point, both in her personal life as well as in her role as the rani. She faced these dual crises with guts and intelligence. There is no

*Rani Lakshmi Bai's statue in Solapur*

doubt that she had been very fond of her stern but sensitive husband, although he was much older than her. She went through all the elaborate rituals of mourning associated with a husband's death, but she did not go through the distasteful and disfiguring ritual of having her head shaved, which widows were expected to do. The rani next threw away the veil and came out of purdah. This was a startlingly bold development and, again, defied tradition. But she had a purpose. She felt that if she was to mean anything to her people she must be much more than a veiled shadow in the background. At this time, they needed a leader, a leader whom they could see and talk to. The rani, however, continued to maintain strict purdah in her dealings with British officials. She talked to them from behind a screen and her attitude with them was stern yet correct.

After she gave up purdah, she began to go on horseback with an entourage through the streets of Jhansi, clad in a Maratha-style sari. The people greeted her warmly whenever they saw her. She also started receiving her subjects every day at a durbar at the palace where she provided them with help and guidance.

In her role as rani, she set about the task of administering the state. She was no novice and over several years, she had involved herself with matters of state and had regular dealings with the *diwan*. But now, after Gangadhar's death, she was manoeuvreing in a difficult situation. She had not been proclaimed the rani as yet and her administrative freedom was restricted. The Jhansi army had not been disbanded and was under her control. On the other hand, the British had taken over the treasury and sealed the prisons.

One cannot help wondering what this extraordinary woman looked like. There are some portraits of her done by contemporary artists. One of these remarkable paintings is at the Victoria and Albert Museum in London and shows a young Lakshmi Bai dressed in fine clothes and wearing her fabulous pearls and diamonds. Along with *kanphool* (long earring), she wears above her forehead a jewelled *kalgi* (aigrette). The face is oval, the eyes large and luminous and the nose delicate and finely chiselled. Altogether a very beautiful woman.

A pen picture has been given by the British writer Meadows Taylor:

> In appearance she was fair and handsome: with a noble presence and figure, and a dignified and resolute, indeed stern expression.... Her dress, though that of a woman, was not the ordinary costume generally worn by females of her class and position in life. Round her neck a diamond necklace sparkled, of not less value than a lakh of rupees, at least. Her bodice, freely opened in front, showed a well-shaped voluptuous bust, and terminated at the waist, which was tightly drawn in by a belt worked over and embroidered with gold, and in it were ostentatiously stuck two elaborately-carved, silver-mounted pistols, of Damascus make, together with a small but elegantly shaped hand-dagger.... Instead of the usual cloth, or petticoat, she wore a pair of loose trousers, from which protruded two small, prettily rounded, bare feet.

Brigadier Sir John Smyth in *The Rebellious Rani* quotes the historical records. 'She was a very handsome woman, about twenty-four years of age, a perfect Amazon in bravery, leading her troops, mounted like a man—just the sort of dare-devil woman that soldiers admire.'

The British started in India as obsequious and lowly traders. It was a story of slow penetration, in which the people of the land themselves helped the foreign intruder. By the early 1800s, they held about one-third of the country, mainly in south and eastern India. After this, the Marathas who were the major power in India, fought till 1818 and the Sikhs till 1849.

It was during the time that Lord Dalhousie was governor-general that a stupendous growth took place with regard to British territory in India. Dalhousie annexed several Indian states under the doctrine of lapse policy, whereby on the failure to produce natural heirs, the sovereignty of the 'dependent' states lapsed to the British government. Eight Indian states, whose rulers had died without leaving a lineal heir, were annexed during Dalhousie's regime.

Although Major Ellis, the assistant political agent at Jhansi and his superior, D.A. Malcolm located at Gwalior, both recommended that the rani's adopted son be recognised as heir, Dalhousie sitting in the Government House in Calcutta, would not agree. The rani then wrote to Dalhousie in December 1853, seeking the government's acknowledgement of the adoption as per the three treaties signed with the British, which clearly stated that adopted sons would be acknowledged as heirs and successors.

She made the important point that adoptions made by the three neighbouring states of Datia, Orchha and Jalaun had been sanctioned by the government and asked how the privilege of adoption could be denied to Jhansi when it was allowed to the others.

Dalhousie turned down the rani's plea and decided to annex the state. He advanced several pseudo-legal arguments in support of this, but these were clearly flawed and misleading. The historian, Sir John Kaye, judged Jhansi as 'the worst of Dalhousie's annexation'.

Town criers went round the various towns and villages of the state announcing the takeover. It was indeed a black day for the people of Jhansi. According to an eyewitness account, the rani is believed to have received Ellis, the agent of Lord Dalhousie, courteously but separated by purdah. When he informed her of the heart-rending news that Jhansi thenceforth ceased to belong to her, that it had been incorporated with the domains of the English, Lakshmi Bai, in a loud yet melodious voice, replied to the agent of the English in these significant words, '*Meri Jhansi nahin dungi*' (I will not surrender my Jhansi).

The rani left the meeting with Ellis in bitter fury and said, 'Whatever happens, the Rani of Jhansi was not born to shed tears'. Brave words, but what indeed could she do? She was a Hindu widow, faced with a hopeless future. A ruler who had lost her throne. A mother with her son's hopes of succession shattered. A woman whose dreams were destroyed.

By now she was losing hope of ever getting justice from the British, but decided that the only way was to send a mission to London. This included the rani's attorney, Kashmiri Mull, and he presented her appeal to the Court of Directors in London. The appeal fell on ears deaf to all considerations, except those of immediate material gain. Her case was finally lost and Dalhousie's word became law.

The British authorities had made decisions regarding the provisions that had to be made for the future. According to the historian G.B. Malleson these provisions 'added meanness to insult'. She was given a pension of five thousand rupees per month, but had to vacate the main palace in the fort and move to another palace in the city. The latter would be considered her private property. She and her retinue were to be exempt from arrest and were not subject to the jurisdiction of British courts. The rani refused to accept the pension.

She quietly left the royal palace in the fort and moved to the city palace. She felt that she had been disgraced and was looked down upon by the neighbouring chiefs of Bundelkhand. She did not do anything rash, as a wing of a native regiment and some artillery were within three marches of the palace and could be destroyed. But deep inside her was an unrelenting determination to retrieve her state. She was reported to have said, 'I will draw my sword, but only when it will be most effective. I will not draw it in vain.'

The British then disbanded the Jhansi state army and the Indian *sipahis* of the Bengal army under British officers who now garrisoned the fort. The cannons on the ramparts of Jhansi fort were rendered unusable and other weapons were confiscated. A Political Officer, Captain Skene, was appointed to administer the state.

The people's hatred for the British was further fuelled by their worsening economic situation. The administrative setup of the maharaja was dismantled by the British as a result of which several people became unemployed. The Jhansi army had already been disbanded and the soldiers were rendered idle. The cumulative effect of all these measures was that the economy of Jhansi suffered, adding to the woes of the people.

Another measure, which was particularly galling to the rani, as to all Hindus, was the introduction of cow slaughter in Jhansi, which had been earlier prohibited.

Further offence was given to the rani and the people by British measures relating to the beautiful Mahalakshmi temple, whose funds were stopped. The rani's protests were in vain.

Meanwhile, the rani continued her daily rides into the town and met the people in the streets and gardens of Jhansi. Her subjects continued to nurse the secret hope that she might yet provide an alternative to British rule. The rani also kept up her daily routine of strenuous physical exercise and training with weapons.

She kept abreast of all the happenings in Jhansi and the other states of Bundelkhand. The rani also had some agents operating in the cantonment. One of these was Moti Bai, who had been a prominent performer in the theatre patronised by the late maharaja. She and another companion sang bhajans to the *sipahis* of the British contingent. They also gleaned much information, which was passed on to the rani. She learnt about the discontent among the *sipahis*, and the happenings in other British army stations.

By June 1857, the nationalists had liberated Delhi and the surrounding areas, as well as the recently annexed kingdom of Awadh, and its capital Lucknow with the exception of the Residency where the British were besieged. This vast tract of liberated territory was not far from Jhansi. Within Bundelkhand itself, several Rajput chiefs including Raja Mardan Singh of Banpur had broken into rebellion.

In Jhansi, neither Skene nor Dunlop of the British garrison took any precautions. On 6 June, a company of the Native Infantry led by a sergeant, Gurbaksh Singh, raised the flag of rebellion and marched into a small fort in the cantonment, called Star Fort, which contained the ammunition and treasure. As they marched to the fort, the citizens of Jhansi cheered and showered them with flowers and garlands.

Skene ordered all seventy British or Anglo-Indian residents to move to the city fort immediately and sent express messages to Gwalior and Kanpur asking for help. Before long all the troops joined the mutiny. They then marched to the jail and released all the prisoners and killed Dunlop and some other British officers in the cantonment.

Captain Gordon and some others then appealed to Lakshmi Bai, the woman they had so grievously wronged, to take charge of the kingdom and save their lives. The rani's cold response was 'You took my kingdom from me under false pretences and now that you cannot keep it, you hand it back to me and ask for my help. My case was decided against me without giving me a hearing. If I now give you any protection, the rebel *sipahis* will destroy me. You have to look after yourselves and save your lives in any way you can.' The rani, however, agreed to shelter the European women and children; this was the utmost she could do, considering her own vulnerable position.

On 8 June, the *sipahis* laid siege to the city fort where all the foreigners had taken refuge. The rebel gunners then brought up two cannons to the fort walls and Captain Skene decided to surrender. The gates were thrown open and the English and Anglo-Indian men, women and children filed out, but they were immediately taken prisoners.

They were then led in a procession through the city to an area called Jokhan Bagh beyond the city walls, where the crowd kept shouting, '*Firangi ko Maro*' (Kill the foreigners). A message then arrived from the leader of the Jhansi mutiny, Rissaldar Kale Khan, ordering that all Europeans should be put to death. A general massacre took place led by Bakshish Ali, the jail *daroga* (prison-warden), who first shot down Captain Skene. The total number of people killed were over sixty.

The massacre at Jhansi was horrible. However, it must be understood that there was much brutality on both sides. By the time the revolt spread to Jhansi, the nationalists had been taught a lesson in savagery by the British. In May 1857, Colonel James Neill, arrived in Benares with the 1st Madras European Fusiliers and unleashed the most hideous terror in the province. To kill an Indian became the 'best sport'.

There has been controversy regarding the rani's precise role in the mutiny and massacre at Jhansi. Contemporary English historians such as Kaye, Malleson, and Forrest maintain that the rani instigated the mutiny at Jhansi and caused the massacre of the English. Later, Indian and English historians re-examined this evidence in depth and their conclusions are quite different from those of earlier writers.

In fact, the rani's own position at this confused time was precarious. If she had given full support to the British, she would have been killed by the rebels; while if she had given succour to the rebels, the British would have been after her blood. The offer of shelter to the women and children, which she made was as much as she could realistically do.

Following the massacre of the Europeans, the mutineers in Jhansi decided to march to Delhi, which was 390 kilometres away. Delhi was the centre of the Revolt and Bahadur Shah sat on the Mughal throne. Soldiers who had mutinied in the surrounding military stations were all converging at Delhi. The *sipahis* at Jhansi were, however, short of funds. They, therefore, went to the palace of the rani with loaded guns and demanded three hundred thousand rupees in cash and supplies of ammunition and guns. They surrounded the palace and their leaders threatened to blow up the building. Their argument was simple; they had rid Jhansi of the British, therefore they must be rewarded.

The rani was in a precarious position because any help to the *sipahis* would ultimately result in a clash with the British, which she wanted to avoid. Under this threat from the soldiers, the rani used all her guile. She told them, 'The British have deprived me of my wealth and left me a pittance. This is no way for gallant soldiers to treat a helpless woman.' In the subsequent parleys, she got them to agree to scale down their demands and finally agreed to pay them one hundred thousand rupees on condition that they leave Jhansi immediately, which they did.

The rani now took over the administration of Jhansi as no other authority existed. As the *bhagwa jhanda* (orange flag) of the Marathas was hoisted on all the state buildings, the people were jubilant. They collected in large numbers at her palace and hailed her as their Maharani.

Administering the state was no simple matter as no organisation existed. The older set-up had been dismantled by the British. To add to the chaos, the *sipahis* had burnt down the administration offices in the city and all the public records and documents essential to any government.

The rani was not an experienced administrator, but she was highly intelligent and learnt fast as she went along. Her top advisors included her father, Moropant Tambe, Diwan Jawahar Singh, Raghunath Singh, Lallu Bakshi, Diwan Lakshman Rao and others. After having taken control of Jhansi, the rani set about mending her fences with the British. She sent a letter to Major Erskine, commissioner, Sagar Division, informing him that the government's *sipahis* had killed all the Europeans. She had no resources to make arrangements for the safety of the district but had saved the town of Jhansi from being plundered. She needed funds and competent government forces to run the district and promised to await further instructions.

Major Erskine, who replied on 2 July, did not doubt the rani's sincerity. He wrote. 'Until a new superintendent arirves at Jhansi, I beg you will manage the district for the British government. When the superintendent takes charge from you, he will not only give you no trouble but will repay you for all your losses and expenses and deal liberally with you.'

Lakshmi Bai's first priority was to re-establish law and order. Dacoits were plundering villages and terrorising people in the area around Barwa Sagar, a town a few kilometres from the capital. The rani went and camped there, personally participated in the raids, destroyed gangs and had them hung or sentenced.

Her second priority was to prepare herself for the coming confrontation with the British. For this purpose, she started organising and equipping an army and contacting other centres of national discontent in order to join hands with them at the opportune moment.

In a few months, she had the administration going smoothly, law courts started functioning, the police operated efficiently and her own money was minted. She took a lot of interest in the state library, the Jhansi theatre, and other cultural activities.

During these days, the rani's daily routine included exercise in the gymnasium and honing her skills with the sword. Every day, she held durbar at which Diwan Lakshman Rao, the chief minister, presented the relevant document to her, which she quickly scanned and issued clear and precise orders.

Twice a week, the rani and her son went in procession to the Mahalakshmi temple, with its lake filled with lotus flowers. One cold wintry evening, while returning from the temple, she saw the poor of the town in coarse cotton garments huddling around hastily built fires in the bylanes of the city. She got down from her horse and asked them all to come to her palace in four days' time. All the tailors of the town were kept very busy for those four days. When the poor in their hundreds gathered in front of the palace, every one of them was handed over a woollen jacket, cap and a blanket.

As things were setting down, a challenge came from the neighbouring states of Orchha and Datia. The Rajputs of Bundelkhand regarded the Marathas as interlopers in their region. Larai Rani (Warrior Queen) who ruled Orchha saw her chance of regaining the territory lost to Jhansi. The British had collapsed and Rani Lakshmi Bai was unprepared for war. Larai Rani was joined by the neighbouring state of Datia and their combined forces totalling 25,000 were placed under the command of her Diwan, Nathe Khan. He sent word to Lakshmi Bai to surrender, to which her reply was 'Do your worst. I will make a woman out of you.'

Lakshmi Bai had few troops and her military stores were poor. Some advisors suggested arriving on a truce but she shamed them all by declaring, 'You are not manly enough to fight, but I, a woman, will teach you how to take on the enemy.'

She then summoned her sardars, among whom were Diwan Jawahar Singh and Raghunath Singh of Nauner. She appealed to them for help with militia and horse. They rallied around and said that with the British thrown out of the state, Jhansi was once again independent and it was their bounden duty to help defend it. In a few days, Jhansi became a vast camp of military leaders, with their men all eagerly waiting for the clash of steel and the smoke of battle. Mardan Singh, the raja of the neighbouring state of Banpur, allied himself with the rani and came with provisions and cannons needed badly by Jhansi.

When news came that Nathe Khan was on the move, Lakshmi Bai assembled her noblemen and fully armed, rode in front of the militia taking their salute. She then summoned Diwan Jawahar Singh who was a Parmar Rajput and the *jagirdar* of a nearby village. She tied an orange string round his wrist, thus entrusting the nobleman with the command of the army and honouring him in the presence of all his peers and the militia. Diwan Jawahar Singh placed his sword at the Rani's feet to show his allegiance to her.

Aware of his strength, the rani let Nathe Khan advance without opposition till he was within range of her cannons on the ramparts of Jhansi fort. The Orchha army thinking that it would be an easy victory, as they had not been opposed, advanced recklessly towards the city. The rani's artillery, under the command of the redoubtable Gulam Ghaus Khan, now opened an intense fire, forcing the invaders to fall back. Nathe Khan decided to be more circumspect and started to concentrate his fire at the six gates of the city with a view to smashing them down and entering the city where the greater strength of his army would be a deciding factor. The Orchha gate suffered heavy damage and there was the fear that it might give way. The rani was constantly at this gate, exposed to the enemy's fire, but her very presence at this vulnerable point was a great inspiration to her men. The damage was repaired and the gate stood. The siege went on for twenty days. The Rani's biggest gun, *Kadak Bijli*, with its greater range, played havoc in the enemy ranks and Nathe Khan's guns were finally silenced and he was forced to withdraw. Jawahar Singh and Raghunath Singh with a large body of cavalry pursued the retreating forces and inflicted heavy damages.

This victory raised the rani's prestige all over Bundelkhand and the neighbouring states viewed her with new-found respect. In Jhansi, the personal regard for her was now sky-high. As we see in this battle and the several subsequent battles against the British, the rani believed in leading by example. She fought alongside her men and was usually where the greatest danger lay. No wonder her men followed her wherever she led them.

Rani Lakshmi Bai had long known that despite her efforts to the contrary, a showdown with the British was inevitable. Consequently, during the peace and tranquillity that followed her destruction of the forces of Orchha and Datia, she did not give up her military preparations.

She re-enlisted in her army all the soldiers from the old Jhansi army and called for volunteers from all over the state. The response was splendid and she raised a force that was estimated at 10,000 to 11,000 men. The majority of these were Bundelas, but also included 1,500 rebel *sipahis* trained in the Company's army. She also had about 1,000 Afghans who, although mercenaries, were fiercely loyal to her. Always unorthodox in whatever she did, she did not make the slightest distinction between Hindus, Muslims or soldiers of any other caste. These troops were trained intensively and the rani personally supervised their daily military exercises and drill.

Her special interest had always been the induction of women as soldiers, another facet of her unorthodox approach. They were taught to ride, shoot, fence and to fire cannons. Several of these women soldiers were later killed on the ramparts of the fort and many more died during the hand-to-hand fighting in the streets of Jhansi.

Diwan Jawahar Singh, who had proved his worth in the earlier engagement against Orchha and Datia, remained in command. He was supported by Diwan Raghunath Singh. The guns were in charge of Lakshmi Bai's famous gunner, Gulam Ghaus Khan, an Afghan mercenary.

*The Fort at Jhansi*

After the British had annexed Jhansi, one of the first things they did was to destroy the guns or make them unusable and bury them under garbage. The rani asked Khuda Baksh, another great gunner, to salvage as many old guns as possible. She also set up foundries to cast new guns. Ammunition and gunpowder was manufactured in large quantities and stored. She also set up factories for the manufacture of rifles, pistols, swords and spears.

Interestingly, in the National Archives, there are intelligence reports by Sir Robert Hamilton, agent to the governor-general, which detail all her war preparations.

Lakshmi Bai had already established contact with other centres of national discontent. She had contacted Tatya Tope, Mardan Singh, and the Raja of Shahgarh, who had rendered invaluable assistance to her in her recent battle against Orchha and Datia, sending men and arms.

Although Lakshmi Bai was making these preparations for war, she kept up her efforts to placate the British. However, she was getting disillusioned and exasperated by their indifference to her appeal. The Rani had realised that the British intended to make her a scapegoat for the mutiny and even the massacre. Jhansi had to be avenged and the victim had to be a person of sufficient importance.

While there was peace in Jhansi from August 1857 to February 1858, most of the country around was aflame and battles raged. By 21 September 1857, Delhi had been reoccupied.

After the British had conquered Upper India again, they could afford to turn their attention to the last stronghold of the Revolt: Central India and Jhansi in particular. By now, the British were in a much stronger position with regard to men and equipment. A lot of time and effort was spent by them in order to assemble the Central India Field Force at Mhow and Sehore, which contained seasoned troops, rushed from Britain. This was a considerable force and its strongest arm was the artillery, which would be most effective against the strength of the Jhansi fortification.

Lord Canning, the new governor-general, deemed the Rani of Jhansi—'the Jezebel of India'—a serious threat and a focal point for the rebels of Central India and therefore, selected a seasoned general to pit against her. This man was Sir Hugh Rose, who although new to India, was one of the most distinguished generals of the British army. He later became a field marshal and was elevated to the peerage as Lord Straithnairn.

Sir Hugh Rose had to cross some mountain passes en route to Jhansi. These were defended again by the gallant rajas of Banpur and Shahgarh. As the British began to ascend into the pass, the raja's guns opened fire and the hills seemed alive with his infantry. The raja's fire increased in intensity and Rose later described it 'as rapid and hot a fire as ever I saw'. The numbers of those killed and wounded increased every moment. General Rose had his horse shot under him and barely escaped with his life. The setback was however, only temporary because Rose had the heavier artillery and managed to push back the Raja's forces and after some intense hand-to-hand fighting, forced him to withdraw. This lost battle had a demoralising effect on the rebels.

Lakshmi Bai had been carefully watching the British movement. In order to make it more difficult for the enemy to collect supplies, Lakshmi Bai cleverly laid waste the countryside around Jhansi; all grass, firewood, vegetables were burnt or moved inside the city. To deny cover to the enemy, trees were cut down, walls and other shelters dismantled. This could have caused considerable embarrassment to the besiegers, but Scindia of Gwalior and the Rani of Orchha came to the rescue and kept the British force abundantly supplied throughout the operation.

Along with Jawahar Singh and Gulam Ghaus Khan, the rani supervised the building of new gun sites and had the existing ones strengthened. As Brigadier Sir John Smyth in *The Rebellious Rani* says, 'How this well brought-up Hindu lady could have learned so much of the fundamentals of war is one of the mysteries which shroud her personality. Like Joan of Arc she had a flair for military leadership and seemed to know instinctively the right course to pursue far better than most of the other more experienced rebel leaders'. Joan of Arc as we know had her voices; Lakhsmi Bai simply had a natural wisdom in these matters.

*A portrait of Maharani Lakshmi Bai*

On 15 March, five days before the enemy arrived, Mardan Singh, and the Raja of Shahgarh rode into Jhansi with soldiers and cannons for the Rani.

Lakshmi Bai finally resolved to fight and she knew it would be a fight to death. She also got the welcome news that Tatya Tope was on the move and was advancing to her aid with a force of 20,000 men.

She assembled her soldiers, townsmen and elders of Jhansi in a town square. There she appeared on a war elephant, dressed like a man and fully armed, with her son, Damodar, sitting by her side. She gave a soul-stirring speech from the howdah of the elephant, which ended with the following words, 'We will be free and independent if we are victorious, if defeated and slain on the battlefield we will have eternal glory.' The people burst into tumultuous cheer and cries of '*Rani Lakshmi Bai Ki Jai*' and '*Jhansi Raj Ki Jai*'. The enthusiasm of the people to fight to death for the freedom of Jhansi was immense.

Lakshmi Bai had sent an appeal for help to her old friends Tatya Tope and Rao Saheb who were waiting not far from the borders of her state with large forces. Tatya Tope responded to such effect that he almost upset the British plans. He marched rapidly with a small force of 900 men towards Kalpi and suddenly swooped on the rajas of Panna and Charkhari who were both staunch allies of the British. This put the British in a quandary.

Sir Rose however ignored the fall of Charkhari to Tatya Tope and arrived at Jhansi with the Central India Field Force on 20 March 1858. Rose, a proven general and a future field marshal, was pitted against a thirty-year-old woman, who had no experience of modern warfare. Though the British army was numerically about equal to the rani's, it was much superior in terms of equipment, supplies and firepower. It was supported by numerous artillery pieces, sappers and miners, and a siege train.

The siege then commenced in real earnest. For seventeen long days, the fire from the British batteries and from the defenders of Jhansi was incessant. Shots and shells were poured into the city and the rani's guns replied powerfully and without respite.

Balwant Parasnis, the eminent historian, who has left a graphic account written in Marathi, says that the enemy continued heavy fire day and night. At night, the cannon balls were an awesome sight as they were hurled into the fort glowing like bright-red live coal. He goes on to add that on 26 March, there was fierce fighting; the sound was incredible, with soldiers shouting, others crying out in agony, with the thunder of cannons and the volleys of muskets. Trumpets and bugles were sounding everywhere. The air was thick with dust and smoke. Many gunners were killed on the ramparts and others immediately stepped forward to take their place. Rani Saheba was everywhere, she looked to everything, issuing orders and inspiring her men with zeal and enthusiasm.

On 27 March, the parapets of the bastion on the mound were damaged and the rani's guns were silenced for a while. But during the night, she had the men and women of Jhansi repair the damages, and next morning, the mamelon was ready for battle once again. As the duel went on day and night, casualties were high among the defenders.

Lakshmi Bai, astride her white charger, was always on the move. She galloped from the city streets to the battlement and back again. She went from rampart to rampart, from bastion to bastion: she was everywhere, moving her soldiers to where she noticed weaknesses, supervising repair work on city walls and, above all, encouraging and inspiring her troops.

By now, however, she was deeply worried that her friends Rao Saheb and Tatya Tope had not come to her aid. They had promised to move in forces but there was no news of them. Without help how would it all end at Jhansi?

It was now the eleventh day of the siege and the continuous bombardment was taking its toll. The mortars lobbing shells at a high trajectory over the fort walls had devastated the city. This uninterrupted cannonade, as well as the courageous and obstinate defence of Jhansi, had caused a great consumption of British ammunition. General Rose therefore, decided to assault the place by escalade or ladders against the fort walls.

*Tatya Tope's soldiery*

The fortunes of Jhansi were at a low ebb. Rani Lakshmi Bai was anxiously scanning the horizon for Tatya Tope's approaching army. On the evening of 31 March, the lookouts on the tower of the fort glimpsed Tatya's army approaching the river Betwa. A wild shout of joy and exultation went up from the defenders. Deliverance was at hand!

Tatya Tope's reputation as a great guerrilla leader and general had been enhanced by his recent victories against General Windham at Kanpur. Tatya was an incorrigible optimist. He was defeated in several battles but the good thing about him was that he never knew when he was beaten, he always came back! But here he was to fight under a major handicap. Although his force numbered 15,000 men, a majority of them were raw recruits, with hardly any training. They were equipped with the old slow firing matchlocks which could not compare with the Enfield rifles of the *sipahis* under British command. The only well trained troops in his army were the rebel Indian *sipahis* and the Afghan mercenaries. They met the enemy charges most bravely, but were outmanoeuvred by Rose's flank attacks. In the continuing battle, Tatya's second line did not hold either, so he set fire to the dry jungle and under cover of the smoke and flames, retreated across the river Betwa.

Rani Lakshmi Bai was stunned and realised that she would have to fight alone. She girded her sword and addressing her troops, said, 'Jhansi looks to nobody for help. We do not need the peshwa's support; we will rely on our own strength for victory. If we have to die then die like heroes.' Her troops had absolute faith in her and everyone vowed to fight to the end.

Gulam Ghaus Khan rearranged his guns, Khuda Baksh and other Bundela and Maratha chiefs strengthened their positions and kept up a fearful fire upon the enemy. The rani went to every post and supervised the defences and both night and day she was with her men.

The increasing fire of the British siege guns had by now damaged the mound or the mamelon, and the breach became bigger. At three in the morning of 3 April, the British troops moved up to their positions to mount the city walls.

The British-led attack was aided by a traitor in the rani's camp and although the Jhansi defenders put up a strong opposition, they managed to force their way in. Parasnis says that the attack would not have succeeded so soon without the help of a traitor, Dulaji Thakur. He was a Bundela Sardar and stopped the firing on receiving a signal in order to enable the storming party to force the breach. For these services, the British later rewarded Dulaji with an estate.

The right attack was to mount the walls by ladders and this is vividly described by Lowe, who accompanied the British force, in his book, *Central India*:

> We had upwards of two hundred yards to march through this fiendish fire, and we did it, and the sappers planted the ladders against the wall in three places for the stormers to ascend, but the fire of the enemy waxed stronger and amidst the chaos of sounds of volleys of musketry and roaring of cannons, and hissing and bursting of rockets, stink-pots, infernal machines, huge stones, blocks of wood and trees,—all hurled upon their devoted heads,—the men wavered for a moment, and sheltered themselves behind stones ... inside bugles were sounding, and tom-toms beating madly, while the cannon and the musket were booming and rattling and carrying death among us fast. At this instant, on our right, three of the ladders broke under the weight of men, and a bugle sounded for the Europeans to retire!

It was in this crisis that the British stormers of the left attack, who had already forced the breach at the mamelon, looked along the wall from the breach and saw the failure of the right attack. They came to the aid of their comrades and charged upon the flank and rear of the Jhansi defenders fighting the right attack.

When the rani realised that the enemy was inside the city walls, a terrible anger seized her. At the head of her 1,000 Afghan regulars, a naked sword in hand she attacked the advancing column of the English. There was fierce hand-to-hand combat, steel clashed against steel, and many, on both sides, were hewn down. The rani was in the thick of the fight and killed many of the enemy herself. This counterattack was so ferocious and unexpected that the English fled.

The rani had checked the enemy, but only for a while. The English were directing an intense fire from a distance at Lakshmi Bai and her men. Bullets were flying everywhere. At this stage, a seventy-five year old Bundela chief, who had accompanied her, realised the danger and pleaded with her to return to the fort. He said, 'If you stay here much longer you will fall prey to the bullets. All city gates have been thrown open. It is pointless for you to sacrifice your life. You must return to the fort at once and work out the next step.' The rani found it difficult to accept this but a moment's reflection showed much sense in it and she returned to the fort to continue the struggle.

The palace had been prepared by the defenders for resistance in the last resort. If the conflict in the streets was severe, at the palace it was desperate. Every room was savagely contested and the rani's devoted men defended it to the end.

She said, 'My people are dying and I have no right to live. The British will never take me alive, even my dead body must not be defiled by their touch. I am going to blow myself up with gunpowder so that no trace is left of me. The rest of you must make your way out of the fort and try and save your lives.'

There was complete silence; then the old chief who had pulled her out of the hand-to-hand fight and brought her back to the palace, went to her and holding her hand, he said, 'Maharani, you must calm down. You are not responsible for the calamity that has befallen the city. It is far better to die fighting than die by your own hand. You must now fight your way out of the city. You must leave tonight and break through the enemy's cordon. Go to Kalpi and meet the peshwa. If in the attempt you die, it will be an honourable death a far better death than the one you are contemplating.'

The old chief had spoken with the authority of a father speaking to his daughter. 'So long as you and your son Damodar are alive and can get to the peshwa, there is always a chance of retrieving our fortunes so that the *bhagwa jhanda* of the Marathas may yet wave again over Jhansi.' The rani with bowed her head and said, 'I have been a blind fool, Baba. You have shown me the way.'

On the night of 4 April, the rani made preparations to leave the fort, a sword and two loaded revolvers in her cummerbund. Seated behind her on the horse and fastened to her back with a silken sash was her son Damodar. She was escorted by 200 fully-armed selected troops, which included some of her loyal Afghans. Her father, Moropant, was part of her escort.

Lakshmi Bai and her party had not gone far before the enemy pickets were roused. Many of her men were killed and in the confusion, but the Rani evading the enemy, rode out of the British line. She was followed by a woman companion and two bodyguards. The four of them and Damodar escaped in the direction of Kalpi.

Rose was astounded and dismayed when he discovered that Lakshmi Bai had escaped. Lieutenant Dowker and a body of horsemen were sent after the rani. He caught up with the rani at Bhandear where she had stopped for food. She was about to leave when Dowker attacked her. But she was too quick for him. With a powerful stroke of her sword, she wounded him severely and he fell into the dust. She would have cut him to pieces but for timely help from one of the cavalrymen. While Dowker was being assisted, the rani and her three attendants made off.

Lakshmi Bai had always been a splendid rider and her horse was a rare animal. Riding hard, she reached Kalpi, the peshwa's headquarters, on 5 April, having traversed 163 kilometres of rugged country in twenty-four hours which, in itself, is a formidable task.

After the fall of Jhansi, it was the turn of the inhabitants of this city to be put through the horror of wholesale slaughter and looting. That night, Godse looked at the city from the rooftop and the whole of Jhansi looked like a cremation ground with fires blazing everywhere.

The loot from the palace, the horses and elephants and other treasure, were auctioned by the British. Scindia of Gwalior delightedly snapped up most of the prized animals and other precious items from the palace.

Lakshmi Bai arrived at Kalpi at midnight with her ten-year-old son strapped behind her. Kalpi, north-west of Jhansi and on the bank of river Yamuna, was a major rebel stronghold and the headquarters of Rao Saheb, Lakshmi Bai's childhood friend. Rao Saheb had assumed the title of Peshwa at the outbreak of the rebellion and was encamped there with his army.

Their meeting the next morning was an embarrassing one for Rao Saheb. It was only because of the ignominious defeat of his army at Betwa, that Lakshmi Bai had lost her capital and was now a fugitive. Her despair was visible as was her anger. Rani Lakshmi Bai said, 'We have not had adequate support from you. Give me an army and I will fight the enemy till I die.' These spirited words uttered by this beautiful and great-hearted woman, who had lost so much left no one unmoved. Present at this time at Kalpi were all her old allies.

At Kalpi under the rani's advice the peshwa's army was reorganised and trained. It was unheard of for women to lead armies and Tatya Tope was appointed commander. The Rani then suggested that the peshwa's army should go forward 70 kilometres towards Jhansi and meet the enemy on favourable ground at the town of Kunch. This site offered several defensive advantages.

As Rose approached Kunch on 5 May, it was a flank attack that he opted for. He made a flank march with his entire force to the north-west of Kunch. A three pronged attack by his army followed, with the huge siege guns directing their fire on the town. The flank attack caused the rebels to draw back although, for a time, Major Orr commanding the Hyderabad Contingent was pushed back by a counterattack of musket fire and Maratha swords. But the well-trained Indian *sipahis* of the British forces forged ahead, despite heavy nationalist artillery and musketry fire. The battle was a short one and Tatya's army was completely defeated. The British were, however, unable to capitalise on this victory as they were too exhausted to keep up the pursuit and Tatya Tope's army was able to withdraw to Kalpi.

The rani, who had participated in the battle, returned to Kalpi with her Jhansi horsemen. She was bitterly disappointed, but was ready to fight on idefinitely and hoped that wiser counsels would prevail in the coming conflict at Kalpi.

The defeat at Kunch led to many recriminations among the peshwa's army. The infantry *sipahis* taunted the cavalry for having abandoned them, whle the cavalry blamed the gunners. The morale of the men had plummeted, but by a stroke of good fortune, the Nawab of Banda arrived at Kalpi at this juncture with 2,000 cavalry and some cannons and infantry. This put a very different complexion on matters and the nawab's efforts, backed by the energy and confidence of the rani, changed the mood from despair to confidence. The *sipahis* who had left Kalpi returned from their hideouts in the villages and forests, and in a few days the army was ready to fight once again.

Kalpi was the last stronghold of the rebels and a major storehouse of ammunition, which they could not afford to lose. Rao Saheb held a council of war at which the rani pointed out that the extensive ravines around Kalpi were a major feature and their plan must take full advantage of them. A skillful battle plan was then drawn up and the Rani was confident that if it was carried out with courage and resolution, victory would be theirs.

Meanwhile, Rose had also strengthened his army. Colonel Maxwell with the Camel Corps, which was composed mainly of Sikhs, had been sent to join Rose. The Camel Corps was to play a crucial role in the ensuing battle.

We will not describe the battle of Kalpi in detail. The main strategy of the nationalists was based on the labyrinth of ravines around Kalpi. Rao Saheb led one wing of the army, while the rani led the other. Rao Saheb's attack from the ravines collapsed and he was driven back to Kalpi.

On the rani's front the whole line of ravines became a mass of fire, the nationalist batteries opened up and their infantry, climbing from below, poured overwhelming musketry fire on the right of the British line. At this stage, the Indians launched a fierce attack on the enemy's right wing and the rani led a brilliant charge. At the head of the Red Cavalry of Gwalior, she charged straight into and through the British line. This sudden onslaught unnerved the British soldiers and their Indian comrades and they were forced to retreat so far back that they reached their own guns and mortar emplacements at the rear. The rani pressed on and got within 20 yards of the British field guns and mortars and outpost tents, and her men sabred the gunners. Another quarter of an hour, and the British would have been massacred.

But Rose, the canny general, had kept the right wing reserve at full strength and not moved any men to support the left wing. When he saw the collapse, he moved swiftly and brought up the Camel Corps and, leading them himself, charged at the advancing rebels. The two sides were locked in close combat but, gradually, the rebel stranglehold was loosened and finally they were pushed back into the ravines. The Sikh soldiers of the Camel Corps had dramatically turned the tide.

The news of Rao Saheb's rout shattered all hopes of victory for the rani and when further resistance was pointless, she and her men also returned to Kalpi. Another battle had been lost. Brigadier Sir John Smyth says: 'If only the other rebel leaders had been of the same calibre as the Rani, who knows what might not have happened.'

That night the rani had to sleep under a tree. It was just as well that she did, as one of the shells from the enemy batteries burst in her room at Kalpi and killed two of her attendants.

Kalpi fell the next day. The morale of the rebels had been broken and there was no resistance. The campaign had now been completed, but before Rose could actually leave, the most shattering news arrived at the headquarters. This news, in the words of a Calcutta newspaper, 'caused throughout India a sensation hardly less than that caused by the news of the outbreak of the mutiny.'

From Kalpi, Rani Lakshmi Bai and Rao Saheb had fled to Gopalpur, 80 kilometres to the south-west of Gwalior. Here they were joined by the Nawab of Banda and Tatya Tope. They had suffered disastrous losses; they had no guns, no equipment and only the remains of an army. Dark clouds of despair hung over them. They wanted to continue fighting but did not know how.

It was then that the Rani pulled them out of the gloom and despondency. She said to them, 'The whole Maratha military tradition has been based on the possession and defence of impregnable fortresses. Shivaji fought the mighty Mughals because he had the strategic forts of Sinhgarh, Raigad and Toran. We just cannot run away, we will be pursued and destroyed. We now need to attack and capture a strong fort and with that as our base; we have to continue our struggle till victory is ours.'

They waited in tense silence for the rani to continue, 'It is the great fort of Gwalior that I have in mind. If we can capture that and win over the Gwalior army to our cause, we will acquire not only military strength but also political influence. We can start anew, we can fight again. Tatya Tope has already visited Gwalior and done much spade work.'

The assembly was electrified. It was a daring and an original suggestion and could have serious repercussions for the British. When the news reached Calcutta that Lakshmi Bai and Rao Saheb were on their way to Gwalior, the British were stunned. Gwalior was in some ways the key to India. Lord Canning telegraphed Sir R. Hamilton, 'If Scindia joins the mutiny, I shall have to pack off tomorrow.' The rani's scheme was accepted and acted upon immediately.

Maharaja Jivaji Rao Scindia was the most important of the Maratha chiefs but he sided with the British, preferring servitude. In the eyes of his army the maharaja was playing a doubtful role.

As the rebel forces advanced towards Gwalior, Scindia marched out with about 8,000 men and several guns and opened fire on the peshwa's forces. This was totally unexpencted and contrary to Tatya Tope's assurances that Scindia's army would not fight. For a while they thought that the volley was really a salute of welcome, till the shells started falling close. The rani ridiculed their expectations and their dismay, and at the head of the cavalry advanced towards the guns. The smoke of the discharge from Scindia's cannons had scarely disappeared when the 2,000 horsemen led by the rani charging at a gallop, carried the guns. Immediately after, the rebels raised a loud cry of *Deen, Deen!* (religion). Scindia's troops responded in the same manner, and fraternised with the peshwa's army. Many went off to eat watermelons in the bed of the Morar River, which was very sensible considering the searing heat of June.

Scindia then fled from the field and did not draw rein till he reached the safety of Agra. He even left his rani and his seraglio behind. The first part of Lakshmi Bai's plan had succeeded admirably. Rao Saheb and his army entered Gwalior in triumph. They took the treasury and Scindia's jewels, the latter said to be of great value. With the money the rebel leaders paid Scindia's army and their own men several months' wages.

With the fall of Gwalior, the peshwa's army had not only acquired the strong fort of Gwalior but also a well trained army and about fifty guns. They had fled in a helpless state from Kalpi, leaving all their equipment and stores behind them. But now they had once more acquired military strength, and equally important, political power.

To celebrate the fall of Gwalior, Rao Saheb held a grand durbar. The festivities went on for days, almost as if liberation from the hated British had already been accomplished. One person was notably absent from the festivities. Rani Lakshmi Bai refused to take part and told Rao Saheb, 'You are wasting time on trivialities and celebrating before victory has been won. If you do not prepare immediately for war, you will destroy our chances.'

As a result, some steps were taken by Rao Saheb but when General Rose reached Gwalior with a reinforced army, the nationalists were inadequately prepared. Rao Sahib realised that he had made a fatal mistake. They now tried to make last minute dispositions of their guns and men. Tatya Tope rushed to see Lakshmi Bai to ask for her advice. He found her furious at the colossal stupidity of her fellow leaders. She said to him, 'The only thing you can do now is to take your troops for one glorious attack on the English without caring for the result. I am ready to do my duty. You do yours. Go ahead and God be with you.'

The rani knew that this was her last battle. She donned her armour, buckled her jewelled sword and mounted her horse. The very sight of her, thus armed, and mounted and wearing her fabulous necklace of pearls around her neck, gave new heart to her men. Many of them carried this last picture of her in their minds and went into battle. She was an inspiring and beautiful woman and she had fought shoulder to shoulder with these men, sharing their dangers, and their fears in battle. They were willing to die with her and swore solemn oaths that they would fight to the bitter end. Raghunath Singh and Munder, one of her woman companions, were by her side.

The contingents of the British moved forward to Kotah-ki-Serai, about 8 kilometres from Gwalior. Here the rani ordered her hidden guns to open fire and at

*The tombs of the Rajas of Jhansi, from 'Le Tour du Monde', 1872*

the same time charged suddenly from behind the hills. This fierce attack surprised Brigadier Smith and he had to withdraw rapidly, losing heavily in the process. At the same time, a body of the rani's cavalry threatened the baggage of the British Indian troops. Matters now looked serious for Smith and he had to send back a detachment to defend the baggage in the rear. He dared not advance that day.

The next morning, Smith advanced again and lured the rebel troops from their sheltered positions into the open plain, where his cavalry could operate freely. The rani advanced to meet them under covering fire from the artillery. The battle raged fast and fierce, but Smith had been reinforced by a squadron of the 8th Hussars. Still the rebels held their ground and the rani led her troops to repeated and fierce attacks, but her ranks were gradually becoming thinner and thinner. She was in the foremost ranks rallying her shattered troops and wielding two swords by two hands, holding the reins of the horse in her mouth. Suddenly she fell from a carbine shot, mortally wounded. The British did not know at what stage of the battle the rani fell, as she was in cavalry uniform and could not be distinguished from the other soldiers. One of her attendants picked her up and carried her to the rear. Her 200 chosen men fought to the last as they had sworn to her and it was only after their deaths that the Hussars broke through. Today, a small temple marks the place near Phool Bagh, where Rani Lakshmi Bai body was said to have been cremated.

The rani had always been haunted by the fear that if killed in battle, her body may fall into the hands of the *melicha* (foreigners) and be defiled by their touch. Her bodyguards, which included Raghunath Singh of Nauner, had this etched on their hearts and in every action they were like her shadow and finally when she did fall they extracted her from the melee.

As soon as it became known that the rani was dead; the rebels lost heart. There were minor engagements between the British and the rebels and desultory fighting continued for two days, but Gwalior fell to the enemy. The remnants of the peshwa's army melted away into the countryside.

General Rose in his battle report paid generous tribute to the rani and compared her to Joan of Arc, a comparison that came naturally to many European observers. He also wrote the sentence that has since become famous, 'Although a lady she was the bravest and best military leader of the rebels.'

# Bibliography


Begum, Nawab Sultan Jahan. *An Account of My Life*, Vol. 1, trans. C.H. Payne. London: John Murray, 1912.

Bhattacharya, Manoshi. *The Royal Rajputs: Strange Tales and Stranger Truths*. New Delhi: Rupa & Co., 2009.

Forrest, Sir George. *A History of the Indian Mutiny*. Edinburgh, London: W. Blackwood, 1904.

Godsey, Vishnu. *Ankhon Dekha Gadar*.

Hardinge, Lord. *My Indian Years, 1910-16*. London: John Murray, 1948.

Hibbert, Christopher. *The Great Mutiny*. New York: Viking Press, 1978.

Holmes, Thomas Rice. *A History of the Indian Mutiny*. London: W.H. Allen, 1888.

Hooja, Rima. *A History of Rajasthan*. New Delhi: Rupa & Co., 2006.

Irvine, William. *Later Mughals*. Calcutta: M.C. Sarkar & Sons, 1922.

Kaye, Sir John William. *A History of the Sepoy War in India, 1857-1858*. London: W.H. Allen, 1864.

Khan, Shaharyar M. *The Begums of Bhopal: A Dynasty of Women Rulers in Raj India*. London: I.B. Tauris, 2000.

Lal Kavi, *Chattraprakash*.

Lang, John. *Wanderings in India: and other sketches of life in Hindostan*. London: Routledge, 1861.

Lowe, Thomas. *Central India during the Rebellion of 1857 and 1858*. London: Longman, Green, Longman, and Roberts, 1860.

Malcolm, Major General Sir John. *A Memoir of Central India*. London: Parbury & Allen, 1823.

Malgaonkar, Manohar. *The Sea Hawk*. Delhi: Vision Books, 1959.

Parasnis, D.B. and C.A. Kincaid. *A History of the Maratha people*. London: Oxford University Press, 1918.

Pogson, Wredenhall Robert. *A History of the Boondelas*. Bundelkhand: B.R. Pub. Corp., rpt 1974.

Preckel, Claudia. *Begums of Bhopal*. New Delhi: Lotus Collection, Roli Books, 2000.

Rousselet, Louis. *India and its Native Princes*. London: Bickers, 1882.

Sarda, H.B. *Maharana Sanga; the Hindupat*. Ajmer: Scottish Mission Industries Company Limited, 1918.

Sarkar, Sir Jadunath. *Fall of the Mughal Empire*. Calcutta: M.C. Sarkar & Sons, 1950.

Sen, S.N. *Eighteen fifty-seven*. Delhi: Publications Division, Ministry of Information & Broadcasting, Govt. of India, 1957.

Smyth, Brigadier Sir John. *The Rebellious Rani*. London: Frederick Muller, 1966.

Somani, R.V. *History of Mewar*. Jaipur: Kitab Mahal, 1976.

Sultaan, Abida. *Memoirs of a Rebel Princess*. New York: Oxford University Press, 2004.

Tamhankar, D.V. *The Ranee of Jhansi*. London: MacGibbon & Kee, 1958.

Tod, Lt Colonel James. *Annals and Antiquities of Rajasthan; Or the Central and Western Rajput States of India*, Vol. 1-3. Ed. and Intro. by William Crooke. Delhi: Low Price Publications, first pub. 1829, rpt 2000.

# Photo Credits

A majority of the images used in this book are in the public domain. We have used only copyright free images mainly for the purpose of elucidating the historical characters, places and important events depicted in this book.

We gratefully acknowledge and list the sources from the Internet that have been very helpful in producing this book:

http://en.wikipedia.org —pp. 4, 6, 14, 19, 21, 30, 37, 38, 43, 46, 48, 50, 51, 58, 68, 75, 78, 83, 84, 100, 107, 108, 114, 124, 131, 133, 145, 149, 158-159, 161, 168, 181, 186, 196

http://commons.wikimedia.org/wiki —pp. 24, 52, 53, 90, 92, 112, 118, 138, 170

http://upload.wikimedia.org/wikipedia/commons —pp. 137, 157

http://horsesandswords.blogspot.in —p. 13

http://indiaexplored.wordpress.com —p. 14

http://travelindore.daccit.net —p. 34

http://grimshaworigin.org —p. 111

http://rlv.zcache.com —p. 137

We are also thankful to the following persons for providing us with copyright free images for this book:

Mr Benoy K. Behl —pp. 20, 136, 140, 142

Shri Mishra, State Museum, Bhopal and Mr Shashank, ADG: DDK, Bhopal —pp. 56-57, 60, 61, 63, 66, 70, 72, 184

Mr E. Jaiwant Paul —pp. 25, 27, 40, 42, 166

# Index

# Index

# Index

*The Gwalior fort, an architectural marvel of India, has witnessed the varying fortunes of the Guptas, Hunas, Kachwahas, Pratiharas, Pathans, Tomars, Mughals, Marathas and the British. The Maan Mandir, Gurjari Mahal, Sas-Bahu temple, Teli-ka-Mandir and several Jain temples—all preserved within the premises of the fort—are some of the landmarks of chivalry and romance left by these rulers. The mighty fort still stands tall, aloof in its majestic splendour.*